Assessment and the
School Library Media Center

Assessment and the School Library Media Center

Editor

Carol Collier Kuhlthau
Associate Professor
School of Communication, Information, and Library Studies,
Rutgers University

Associate Editors

M. Elspeth Goodin
and
Mary Jane McNally

1994

LIBRARIES UNLIMITED, INC.
Englewood, Colorado

LIBRARIES UNLIMITED, INC.
P.O. Box 6633
Englewood, CO 80155-6633
1-800-237-6124

Project Editor and Proofreader: Tama J. Serfoss
Interior design and font selection: Kay Minnis
Layout: Alan Livingston
Editorial assistance: Susie Sigman

Library of Congress Cataloging-in-Publication Data

Assessment and the school library media center / editor, Carol Collier
   Kuhlthau ; associate editors, M. Elspeth Goodin and Mary Jane
   McNally.
    xi, 152 p. 17x25 cm.
    Includes bibliographical references and index.
    ISBN 1-56308-211-X
    1. Library orientation for school children--United States.
   2. Instructional materials centers--United States--User education.
   3. Searching, Bibliographical--Ability testing. 4. Information
   retrieval--Ability testing. I. Kuhlthau, Carol Collier, 1937- .
   II. Goodin, M. Elspeth. III. McNally, Mary Jane.
   Z711.2.A84   1994
   025.5'678'0973--dc20   94-27290
                                                    CIP

Contents

Introduction

During the publication of the 1993 edition of School Library Media Annual, *the editors realized that while an entire section of SLMA was devoted to the topic of assessment, library media specialists needed and were demanding even more attention to the topic. After pulling the articles at hand and searching through the literature for other quality articles, the editors now present what they believe is a fine addition to the literature.*

Assessment of student learning, the measuring of students' progress and performance, is an important concern for library media specialists, and the problem is being given serious attention across disciplines and at all levels of education. As we progress through the nineties, the question, "What makes an educated person in the information age?" remains unsolved. But while a clear consensus has not been reached, new curriculum statements in mathematics, science, social studies, and language arts state as objectives higher-level thinking, problem solving, and information use skills. Process skills that enable lifelong learning in a complex, rapidly changing, technological society are coming to the fore. The library media center is a critical component of the information age school in providing students with the resources, technology, and processes for learning from information. But how is such learning measured? How do we know students have understood deeply and acquired transferable skills? These questions need serious consideration to enable library media specialists to be responsive to the public they serve.

This book is a compilation of articles addressing the issue of assessment of library media services from a number of different perspectives. All of the authors agree that better measures of assessment are needed. The newer methods being developed and implemented are particularly suited to the type of learning taking place in library media centers.

George F. Madaus and Ann G. A. Tan overview the history of testing and assessment in American education. They document the extraordinary growth of standardized testing beginning in 1943 and the reasons behind this growth. They describe the current status of testing and the rise of the assessment movement, and they discuss the impact of testing on students, teachers, and schools. "Testing and assessment have important roles to play in education; what we need for the remainder of this century—and into the next—are ways to properly evaluate, prioritize, and monitor those roles."

Mary M. Jackson analyzes the questions related to library information skills on the most commonly used standardized tests. She notes that while new measures of assessment are clearly needed and are being developed, today's reality is that standardized tests are a primary means for assessing student learning in library media centers. She describes a paradigm shift in library media programs from library location skills to information-processing skills. She provides an assessment of library information skills on three standardized tests and concludes that in many ways these tests have been adapted to better assess information-processing skills.

However, she finds that these tests reduce assessment to short questions and answers that cannot fully reflect the complex mental processes engaged in information use.

Robert E. Berkowitz clearly states the critical problem before library media specialists, establishing accountability to gain the support of administrators. He warns that, "If library media specialists are to fulfill their mission, they must convince those who make decisions of their clear and valuable impact on student learning." He refers to the guidelines in *Information Power*, which call for a new system of program evaluation and show that new methods of gathering data are needed to demonstrate the positive relationship between the library media program and student success. Berkowitz challenges library media programs to develop measures of effectiveness that show their impact on school goals and student achievement, attitudes, and behaviors. He explains that library media programs go beyond providing resources and teaching location and access skills. He points out that, "Library media specialists have a unique perspective that instruction is a series of information-based problems to solve." He states that process-oriented instruction is at the heart of learner outcomes. When process and content are connected, students demonstrate competency through performance-based objectives. Berkowitz offers some practical steps for developing measures of effectiveness for assessing student learning in library media centers.

As the instructional role of the library media specialist continues to evolve, new intervention and evaluation strategies will be created. In an award-winning paper, Daniel Callison proposes expanding the role of evaluation to address the critical thinking curriculum. He asserts that, "If evaluation is limited to materials selection and does not include evaluation of student information use, the school library media specialist cannot claim to be an educator on par with the classroom teacher." He suggests that self-assessment, process assessment, and product assessment are all needed to determine what worked and what can be improved.

Critical thinking is central to the library research process. As the process of library research draws to a close, students may be guided in self-assessment that deepens learning and facilitates transference to other information-seeking situations. Carol Collier Kuhlthau recommends some qualitative strategies for helping students assess their own research process using time lines, flowcharts, conferences, and summary statements.

Delia Neuman describes the state-of-the-art in qualitative evaluation of student learning and explains important implications for application by library media specialists. Beginning with a discussion of the criticisms of standardized testing that generated the alternative assessment movement, she presents the theoretical assumptions of alternative assessment, the emerging body of research and practice in specific alternative assessment models, and criticisms of alternative assessment. Neuman recommends application of the alternative assessement approach for library media services and suggests a context library media specialists might adopt to foster the productive use of alternative assessment. She explains that the process-oriented approach of alternative assessment relies on three core strategies: (1) observing students working, (2) interviewing students about their changing perceptions and understandings, and (3) analyzing the documents the students prepare. Involving students in reflective interviews based on their projects and portfolios provides the basis for assessment.

Barbara K. Stripling discusses planning the assessment of student performance as a critical step in the instructional design process. She recommends authentic assessment and explains three levels of involvement by the library media specialist at the assessment of student performance step. Four main categories of authentic assessment identified are: tests, portfolios, performances, and personal contact with the student.

Carol A. Meyer clarifies the difference between *authentic assessment* and *performance assessment*, two terms that are often used interchangeably but do not mean the same thing. She offers clear examples for distinguishing the two terms and criteria for determining authenticity. She identifies implications for educators that may also be applied to library media specialists.

In a second article, Barbara K. Stripling provides a comprehensive description of authentic assessment, beginning with its origin and impetus in the current restructuring movements. She further explains four types of authentic assessment that promote student motivation and thinking skills and offers offers extensive examples of activities for assessing the information processing skills of recalling, explaining, analyzing, challenging, and transforming. Stripling presents a case study that clearly demonstrates the role of the library media specialist in authentic assessment to facilitate higher-level thinking. She provides a practical framework for developing the role of the library media specialist as evaluator of process and product.

Daniel Callison, in his second article, describes portfolio assessment and its potential for library media programs. He explains that new curriculum designs that emphasize constructing meaning, problem solving, higher-level thinking, and the use of collaboration and group work require new forms of assessment. Portfolios establish a record of student growth and allow for comparisons at different stages in the learning process. Using examples of students' emergent abilities in reading and writing, Callison lays the foundation for developing portfolio assessment for information skills. He advocates the development of methods that incorporate student reflection into the assessment process.

The last two articles describe how two school districts have implemented new approaches to assessment. In the first example, Nora Redding describes how a Colorado school district established ambitious learning outcomes to prepare students for the 21st century, then used a framework developed at a nearby educational laboratory as a model to create appropriate assessment criteria and tasks. The district has taken on the mission of graduating students who are: (1) self-directed learners, (2) collaborative workers, (3) complex thinkers, (4) quality producers, and (5) community contributors. Creating the ability to document when students achieve these outcomes required a radical change in assessment.

In the second example, the library media center and the library media specialist play an integral role in implementing the new approach to assessment. Willa Spicer and Joyce C. Sherman describe a sixth-grade performance assessment program designed to measure the students' ability to research and present information. The program is based on close collaboration between the classroom teacher and the library media specialist. Outside assessors representing local businesses, district parents and teachers, administrators and teachers from other districts, and students from local colleges are called upon to evaluate the students' projects.

Taken together, these articles provide a comprehensive overview of the state of assessment in school library media programs. The important issue before the community of library media specialists is one of identifying and implementing assessment techniques that reveal the impact of school library programs on student learning.

1

The Growth of Assessment

 George F. Madaus and Ann G. A. Tan

Education in the United States has undergone extraordinary changes during ASCD's first half-century. Arguably, one of the most radical and influential changes concerns the role of standardized tests. In 1943, when ASCD (Association for Supervision and Curriculum Development) was new, most teachers and children considered standardized achievement tests innocuous. As one observer put it:

> [Everyone] knew virtually nothing was ever done with the results. When the teacher spent the morning giving a [standardized] test, it was an easy morning for him or her, and a not unpleasant one for most of the pupils. Such tests were much less threatening to the children than a test prepared by the teacher on which a grade might depend (Travers 1983, 145).

Although testing had been used as a policy tool in American education at the local level since at least the 1840s (Tyack and Hansot 1982; Massachusetts Historical Society Documents 1845-46; White 1888; Madaus and Kellaghan 1992) and in New York with its Regents Examination since the 1870s, the nature and magnitude of test use changed dramatically after World War II. Each succeeding decade witnessed an inexorable shift—at first subtle, then dramatic—in the importance of testing as a major tool of educational policy.

The passage in 1958 of the National Defense Education Act (NDEA) marked the emergence of testing as a tool in the national policy arena. By the late '60s, as one key observer stated, standardized test results were "employed to make keep-or-kill decisions about educational programs. Big dollars were riding on the results of achievement tests .... The days of penny-ante assessment were over." (Popham 1983, 23). A decade later, many states discovered the policy potential of testing and linked standardized test performance to decisions about student graduation, promotion, and placement (Madaus and McDonagh 1979; Madaus 1983). In the 1980s, states expanded the use of student test results in several ways: evaluating teacher and school effectiveness, putting school systems into receivership, and allocating resources to schools and districts (Haertel 1989; Madaus 1985, 1988). And in this, the last decade of the 20th century, clarion calls are heard from many, including President Bush, to create a national testing system, geared to "world class standards." In its seminal report, the National Council on Education Standards and Testing (NCEST) argued that "standards and assessments linked to the standards can become *the cornerstone of the fundamental, systemic reform necessary to improve schools*" (NCEST 1992, 5; emphasis added).

Over the past fifty years, we have seen U.S. educational testing proliferate into many important, interesting applications—test use in the guidance movement, creativity testing, the development of test standards and codes of testing by professional organizations, the establishment of the National Merit Scholarship Corporation, test use in mastery learning, school effectiveness indicators, and criterion/curriculum-referenced testing. On the technical front, we witnessed the development and use of normal curve equivalents (NCEs), National Assessment of Educational Progress (NAEP) scaling, and item response theory (IRT). As well, we have seen declines in the scores of U.S. students on the Scholastic Aptitude Test (SAT). Testing has also been part of important debates in education, such as the IQ controversy, the influence of teachers' expectations (known as "Pygmalion in the classroom"), and "Truth in Testing" legislation. More recently, we have seen the emergence of new developments, such as the theory of multiple intelligences and "authentic" assessment. However, we believe that the main testing story of the past fifty years is its evolution as a social technology, first to inform, and eventually to implement national educational reform policy. This chapter documents and describes the extraordinary growth of standardized testing as a policy mechanism and the reasons behind this growth, from 1943 through the present.

We first present a brief history of how changes in the technology of testing and beliefs about teaching and learning before the 1950s influenced testing after World War II. Next, we describe some indicators of the growth of testing over the past fifty years and offer an explanation for this remarkable growth. We then describe the present status of testing and the rise of the assessment movement. Finally, we attempt to predict the future of standardized testing in American education.

CHANGES IN THE TECHNOLOGY
OF TESTING BEFORE 1943

Testing was first introduced as a policy mechanism in China in 210 BC to select virtuous men for civil service positions. Since then, there have been only three ways to test or examine people—by requiring them to:

1. Supply an oral or written answer to a series of questions (e.g., essay or short-answer questions or the oral disputation) or produce a product (e.g., a portfolio of artwork, a research paper, or an object, such as a chair or a piece of cut glass).

2. Perform an act to be evaluated against criteria (e.g., conduct a chemistry experiment, read from a book, repair a carburetor).

3. Select an answer to a question or posed problem from among several options (e.g., the multiple-choice or true-false item).

Each testing method has built-in constraints inherent in its design. Over the centuries, test users have had to grapple with these constraints, and their solutions help explain the evolution of standardized testing as a major social technology in the educational policy arena in the United States. An apt metaphor to use in problem solving in any technological area comes from the military: *the reverse salient in an expanding military front*. In World War I, advances along the battle line were often uneven. Before a general advance could continue, any reverse bulge or "salient" in the front line had to be eliminated. Technological systems, like an advancing military front, also develop unevenly. Some components of the system fall behind others, acting as a drag on the entire system by functioning inefficiently, malfunctioning, or adding disproportionately to costs. Inventors such as Edison, the Wright brothers, Bell, and Sperry concentrated their efforts on eliminating "reverse salients" impeding the advance of already existing technologies (Hughes 1989). Similar changes have occurred in the technology of testing over the centuries.

The history of testing in Europe and the United States shows that changes or adaptations in testing technology were directed at making testing more efficient, manageable, standardized, objective, easier to administer, and less costly in the face of increasing numbers of examinees. For example:

- In the 18th century, the oral disputation—the predominant assessment technology of the time—aimed at assessing universal rhetorical skills that could be brought to bear on any subject, was supplemented by the written exam to more *efficiently* assess mathematics, a new curricular offering in the university (Hoskins 1968; Montgomery 1967; Madaus and Kellaghan 1992).

- The same century saw the innovation of assigning quantitative marks to performance, because examiners tended to be subjective and partial in their *qualitative* judgments of students' oral disputations and written examinations. This shift permitted the seemingly more "objective" ranking of examinees and the averaging and aggregating of test scores (Hoskins 1968; Madaus and Kellaghan 1992).

- In 1845 Horace Mann supplanted the oral exam in the Boston Public Schools with the written essay exam. Although Mann had political reasons for making the change, he also recognized that written examinations allowed examiners to administer *uniform* examinations to a rapidly expanding student body in much *less time*, producing *comparable results* across students that were not previously possible with oral examinations (Madaus 1990).

- In the first decade of the 20th century, the short-answer-supply mode appeared. Samuelson (1987) named Fredrick Kelly as the inventory of the multiple-choice item in 1914 (though Thorndisk and Lohman 1990 credit the Chinese with the development and use of the selection/multiple-choice test). The development of short, easily scored test items occurred partially in response to the Starch and Elliott (1912, 1913) studies, which showed that the marks assigned to essay questions were highly unreliable, and partly in response to the growth of the scientific management movement's adaptation to education, which required that growing numbers of children be tested to measure a district's efficiency (Callahan 1962).

- In 1917, Otis's development of a group-administered IQ test, the Army Alpha, overcame the administrative, scoring, and cost limitations associated with the individually administered Binet. Once again the sheer number of examinees that needed to be tested—almost 2 million recruits—demanded a technology that was more efficient, cheaper, more manageable, and easier to score and record (Sokal 1987).

- In 1926, the College Entrance Examination Board adopted the multiple-choice format and dropped the writing component of the SAT in 1937, partly because of the cost of scoring and to permit greater variety of test content (Angoff and Dyer 1971).

One important post-World War II technological development—the invention by Lindquist of the high-speed optical scanner—further facilitated the deployment of the large-scale, low-cost, multiple-choice testing programs of the '60s, '70s, and '80s. (At the beginning of the 1990s, a reaction against these cheap, efficient, administratively convenient, multiple-choice testing programs set in—a development we discuss later in this chapter.)

Before leaving this pre-1950 history of testing, we should mention a widely held belief and a momentous technical development that became closely related: the recurring, strong, traditional notion that all students could learn if properly taught and the invention of *ability* or *intelligence* tests in the late 19th century.

The Belief That All Children Can Learn

Since at least the 15th century, many people have believed that if teachers taught correctly, pupils should surely learn. Coupled with this belief was the practice of using examination results as a mechanism for holding teachers accountable to ensure that students obtained certain educational outcomes. For example, a 1444 contract between the town fathers of Treviso and its schoolmaster stipulated that the schoolmaster's salary would be linked to the pupils' level of attainment—measured by a *viva voce* examination—on the grammar curriculum of the time (Aries 1962). This "payment by results" provision of the Treviso contract is one of the earliest examples—predated perhaps only by the Chinese mandarin civil service examinations—of the use of the technology of testing as a form of centralized, hierarchical, managerial control. Indeed, much of the mandated standardized testing that goes on today is essentially bureaucratic rather than educational in its sponsorship, character, and use (Madaus and Kellaghan 1992).

The assumption that all students would learn if properly taught continued to be common both in Britain and America, at least through the first half of the 19th century, when schools dealt with small numbers of pupils. For example, consider the 1845 letter from Horace Mann to Samuel Gridley Howe on how to use results from the newly introduced, printed, written examination in the Boston public schools:

> Some pieces should be immediately written for the papers, containing so much of an analysis of the answers, as will show that the pupils answered common and memoriter questions far better than they did questions involving a principle; and it should be set forth most pointedly, that in the former case, the merit belongs to the scholars, in the latter the demerit belongs to the master. All those abominable blunders which are even more to be condemned for their numbers than for their enormity; orthography, punctuation, capitalizing and grammar are the direct result of imperfect teaching. *Children will not learn such things by instinct. They will not fail to learn them, under proper instruction . . . . One very important and pervading fact in proof of this view of the case, is the great difference existing between schools, on the same subject, showing that children could learn, if teachers had taught* (Massachusetts Historical Society Documents 1845-1846; emphasis added).

This remarkable quote has a distinctly contemporary ring to it: the publication in the newspapers of test results for political and bureaucratic purposes; the use of test results to describe curricular outcomes and to hold teachers and school accountable for poor results; and the distinction between lower- and higher-order thinking skills in the curriculum and examinations.

The belief that all students could learn if properly taught, however, was seriously eroded in the face of poor student performance when compulsory attendance, new immigration, and the abolition of child labor in the latter part of the 19th century forced educators to deal for the first time with a large and very diverse population of students.

The Development of Intelligence and Ability Tests

Until the end of the 19th century, tests or examinations were what we now call "achievement" tests. They concentrated on a syllabus, curriculum, or craft. The advent of the IQ testing movement in the latter part of that century altered testing forever. Proponents of mental testing claimed, and it was widely believed, that testing could do more than assess what people learned: it could now measure they underlying mental ability or intelligence (Madaus 1990). This development had profound effects on the ways in which educators came to view school organization, classroom grouping, and the capacity of individual students to learn and profit from instruction.

Thus, by 1918 the ability level of students was used to "explain" why many students could not be expected to do well. For example, one prominent educator of the time argued that "unsatisfactory school results is [sic] to be traced to the native limitations in the ability of the child or to the home atmosphere in which the child grows up" (Judd 1918, 152). "Scientific" tests of both achievement and "intelligence" quickly began to serve as selection devices to identify talent and to place students in the "proper" curriculum for their ability level. Curriculum became differentiated according to student "ability" level, often with disastrous consequences for minorities and non-English speakers.

The interpretation of "intelligence" test scores as reflecting some sort of innate ability overlooked the fact that Binet's original intent was to identify persons in need of specialized instruction. Binet's tests were samples of ability, and "to interpret them as measures of 'general intelligence' was a flagrant overgeneralization" (Snow and Yalow 1982, 505). Nonetheless, such overgeneralizations have been made repeatedly over the decades. It reemerged with a vengeance in the 1960s with the publication of Arthur Jensen's (1969) controversial article, "How Much Can We Boost IQ and Scholastic Achievement?" Jensen argued that "genetic factors are strongly implicated in the average Negro-white intelligence difference" (82). Another controversial article along the same lines of Jensen's was Richard Herrnstein's "IQ." Rebuttals and counter arguments to Jensen's thesis quickly followed and continued in to the 1980s (see Block and Dworkin 1976). Stephen Jay Gould, for example, in *The Mismeasure of Man* (1981), addressed what he saw as the twin fallacies underlying Jensen's hereditarian IQ argument: "reification"—the assumption that test scores represent a single, scalable thing called general intelligence; and "hereditarianism"—equating "heritable" with "inevitable" and the confusion of within- and between-group heredity.

In the 1980s, Carroll raised a variation on the controversy when he pointed out that many of the more difficult tasks used in the NAEP reading assessment—tasks measuring so-called higher-order thinking—resemble tasks found on tests of verbal and scholastic aptitude. While he recognizes the argument might be unpopular, he wondered if those NAEP exercises were a measure of national verbal ability, and if they were, then he worried that the research literature did not hold out much hope of improvement given present educational methods (Carroll 1987).

The School Effectiveness Movement

The idea that all students could learn if properly taught lay dormant from the first decade of this century until Jerome Bruner (1966), John Carroll (1963), and Benjamin Bloom (1968) revived the idea in the 1960s. Beginning in the late '70s, the school effectiveness movement linked the reemergence of the idea that all students could learn with another popular development of the mid-'60s related to testing: the expectancy, self-fulfilling prophecy, or "Pygmalion" effect (Rosenthal and Jacobson 1968). In one of the most oft-cited works in education (Wineburg 1987), Rosenthal and Jacobson concluded that the provision of *false ability*-test information to teachers had led to an improvement in pupils' measured scholastic *ability*. Despite being strongly criticized on statistical and design grounds, and years of failure on the part of hosts of researchers to demonstrate a similar effect, Rosenthal and Jacobson's Pygmalion effect nonetheless became widely accepted as a social truth (Kellaghan, Madaus, and Airasian 1982; Wineburg 1987). A central tenet of the school effectiveness movement was that effective schools made it clear to both teachers and students that all students could and were expected to learn (e.g., Edmonds 1980). As Wineburg (1987) observed, the road to academic success "was paved with the power of positive thinking" (35).

A similar belief in the power of positive expectation can be found in the rhetoric of the 1990s reform movement, with the assertion that all students can attain "world class standards" in the five curricular areas covered by the National Goals—math, science, English, history, and geography (Madaus and Kellaghan 1991; U.S. Department of Education 1991). This expectation would be backed up by a high-stakes accountability system that would monitor the progress of schools and individuals toward the attainment of these world class standards.

Let us turn now to the phenomenal growth of testing over the past fifty years.

THE GROWTH IN TESTING, 1950 TO 1990

In 1930, an estimated 5 million standardized educational tests were administered annual (Strenio 1981. Unfortunately, there is little documentation on Strenio's growth estimates.) By 1990, it was conservatively estimated that each year elementary and secondary students take 127 million separate tests as part of standardized test batteries mandated by states and districts [National Commission on Testing and Public Policy (NCTPP) 1990]. At some grade levels, a student might have to sit for seven to twelve such tests a year.

The commission found that testing was generally heavier for students in special education or bilingual programs. Many indicators show the enormous growth of testing over the past fifty years: the growth in the number of state testing programs from 1960 onward; sales of tests and scoring services; citations in *Education Index*; and citations in *Educational Leadership*. Incidentally, growth in U.S. testing programs is also shown by changes in the *Mental Measurement Yearbooks*, from the first edition in 1938 to the tenth edition in 1989 (Buros 1938; Conoley 1989).

Growth in State-Mandated Testing Programs

Figure 1.1 shows a steady rise in numbers of state-mandated *assessment programs*, from one in 1960 to thirty-two by 1985. The rise in numbers of *minimum competency testing programs* at the state level has been even more dramatic: from one such program in 1972 to thirty-four programs by 1985. By 1990, every state had some kind of mandated testing program. Naturally, with every state mandate, the number of students tested—and hence the number of tests administered—increased (NCTPP 1990).

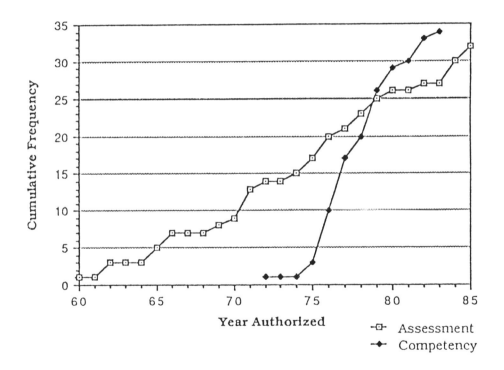

Fig. 1.1. States Authorizing Minimum Competency and Assessment Programs. From Office of Technology Assessment: U.S. Congress (1987).

Growth in Test Sales

The second growth indicator is that of the increase in the *reported* dollar volume of sales of tests and testing services at the elementary and secondary levels (referred to in the industry as the Elhi market). Figure 1.2 shows the sales figures for standardized tests for the Elhi market, from 1955 through 1986, and those sales adjusted for inflation using the 1988 Consumer Price Index (NCTPP 1990). These data were taken from *The Bowker Annual* (1970-1987). *Bowker* gets its sales figures from the Association of American Publishers' (AAP) *Industry Statistics Report*. See Haney, Madaus, and Lyons (1993) for a more detailed description of the *Bowker* figures.

Figure 1.2 shows a dramatic growth rate since 1955, of almost 400 percent, in the real dollar volume of sales of tests and testing services. Sales rose from less than $30 million in 1955 to more than $100 million by 1986 (1988 dollars). Actual revenues from sales of tests and related testing services may be as much as four or five times higher than those reported in *Bowker*—somewhere on the order of half a billion dollars (not shown in figure 1.2). Further, the increased revenues of the testing industry are due more to the increased volume of testing than to increases in the costs of tests or test-scoring services (Haney, Madaus, and Lyons 1993).

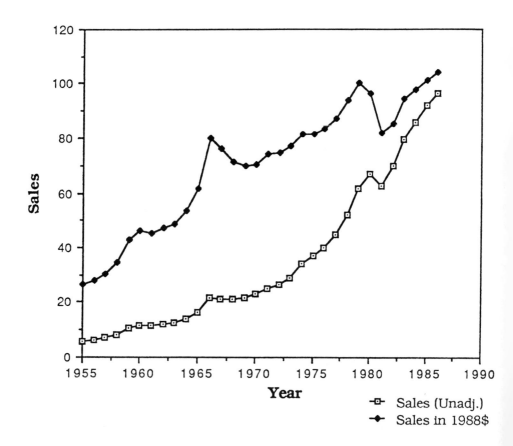

Fig. 1.2. Test Sales in Unadjusted and Adjusted Millions of Dollars. From *The Bowker Annual*, 1970-1987.

Growth as Reflected in the *Education Index*

An indirect indicator of the growth in testing developed by Haney and Madaus (1986) charts the number of citations in the *Education Index* under the rubric "tests and scales" (as indicated by number of column inches) from 1930 onward. For comparative purposes, and of interest to ASCD members, Haney and Madaus also charted the citations under the "curriculum" rubric.

In terms of the sheer *numbers* of articles under the various testing rubrics found in *Education Index*, there were 179 articles in the edition covering the years 1941-44; by the 1990-91 edition, the number had swelled to 728; the number of articles peaked between July 1984 and June 1985 at 1,154 titles.

Figure 1.3 shows that the average annual number of column inches devoted to citations concerning *curriculum* increased only modestly over the past sixty-one years—from 50 to 100 inches per year in the 1930s and 1940s to only 100 to 150 in recent years. In contrast, column inches devoted to *test and scales* have increased dramatically, from only 10 to 30 in the 1930s and 1940s to well over 300 in 1990-91. (The correlation between column inches devoted to testing and year is whopping 0.91.) This index is admittedly crude; but the data certainly indicate that the prominent of testing, as represented in the education literature, has increased dramatically, particularly since the mid-1960s.

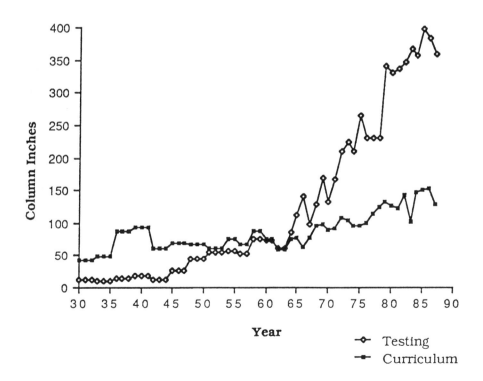

Fig. 1.3. *Education Index* **Listings Under Testing and Curriculum.** From *The Bowker Annual*, 1970-1987.

Growth as Reflected in *Educational Leadership*

In the decade of the '40s, *Educational Leadership* published a total of five articles with the rubrics "evaluation," "test," or "measurement" in the title. The number of articles, as well as the rubrics relating to testing, grew to more than ninety articles during the decade of the '80s. The first two years of the '90s have already seen thirteen such articles.

The phenomenal growth of minimum competency testing (MCT) is clearly documented by coverage in *Educational Leadership*. For example, the cover of a 1977 issue had two maps of the United States, the first showing states that had MCT programs in January, the second showing that ten additional states had programs the following September. Between October 1978 and May 1979, *Educational Leadership* published eleven articles dealing with MCT, compared to one article between the same months for 1976 to 1977.

CHANGES IN TEST USE

The conclusion seems inescapable: educational testing has expanded dramatically over the life of ASCD, in terms of both volume and societal importance. But growth is only part of the story; the uses to which test results were put also have changed dramatically. The NCTPP (1990) noted that dramatic growth in testing since the 1950s was coupled with the trend of greater reliance on test results to make critical decisions about children, such as:

- Entry to and exit from kindergarten

- Promotion from grade to grade

- Placement in remedial programs

- Graduation from high school

Further, there was a dramatic increase in the use of students' scores to hold school systems, administrators, and teachers accountable.

In 1992, as previously noted, the NCEST endorsed the use of assessments to monitor individual and system progress toward the national education standards and:

- to exemplify for students, parents, and teachers the kinds and levels of achievement that should be expected;

- to improve classroom instruction and improve the learning outcomes for all students;

- to inform students, parents, and teachers about student progress toward the standards;

- to measure and hold students, schools, districts, states, and the Nation accountable for educational performance; and

- to assist in education program decisions to be made by policymakers (NCEST 1992).

Thus, not only has the volume of testing increased, but testing has become a high-stakes policy tool looming ominously over the lives of many educators and children, influencing what is taught and how, and what is learned and how (NCTPP 1990).

In addition, the costs to taxpayers for state and local testing have also increased. The NCTPP estimates annual costs of between $725 and $915 million and points out that classroom time taken to prepare students specifically for mandated tests could be put to any number of alternative instructional uses. For example, one study of "opportunity costs" in mathematics concluded that teachers who spend the bulk of their effort teaching to the yardstick of present standardized tests sacrifice the intellectual engagement that students need to develop the kind of mathematical abilities recommended by the National Council of Teachers of Mathematics (Romberg, Zarinnia, and Williams 1989).

REASONS FOR THE GROWTH IN TESTING

What caused the rapid growth in testing and the attendant shift to high-stakes policy uses of test results? Four broad social forces at work during the past fifty years help explain the transformation of testing today (Haney, Madaus, and Lyons 1993).

- Recurring public dissatisfaction with the quality of education in the United States and efforts to reform education.

- A broad shift in attention from focusing on the inputs or resources devoted to education toward emphasizing the outputs or results of our educational institutions.

- An array of legislation, at both federal and state levels, promoting or explicitly mandating standardized testing programs.

- Bureaucratization of education and schooling.

These broad forces are by no means independent. For example, a specific episode of public dissatisfaction with education often leads to legislation mandating new tests, which in turn focuses public attention on outcomes of schooling, or at least on test scores; and legislation and testing are implicated in the increased bureaucratization of education. Despite such interdependencies, for ease of discussion we treat these forces separately.

Dissatisfaction with Education and Efforts at Reform

Over the past fifty years, there have been at least six major cycles of educational dissatisfaction and reform, each of which has contributed to the growth of standardized testing either by using test results to inform policymakers about the state of education or as a mechanism of policy aimed at transforming education.

The first cycle began with the Sputnik launching in 1957, which sparked national concern about U.S. science, math, and technical education in general and our military and technological competitiveness with the Soviet Union in particular. In response, the U.S. Congress passed the National Defense Education Act.

The second cycle of dissatisfaction and reform began with the compensatory education and civil rights movements of the 1960s. First, advocacy groups seeking aid for their constituents pointed to glaring disparities between the standardized test performance of their constituents and that of middle-class students. Second, in the early 1960s, with the publication of the famous *Coleman Report* (Coleman et al. 1966), policymakers began to use standardized test results not only for information about the condition of American education in general, but also eventually as the yardstick against which to judge the impact of compensatory programs, such as Head Start and Title I (Madaus 1985). These movements also led to important legislation, which had a serious impact on testing and the testing industry.

The third cycle was marked by the furor in the 1970s over national declines in SAT scores. These declines raised great concern over the quality of education in the United States and contributed to the rise of the MCT movement.

The 1980s saw the next wave of reform reports, the most famous of which was *A Nation at Risk* (National Commission on Excellence in Education 1983a). This cycle of dissatisfaction and reform efforts rekindled concerns over U.S. competitiveness, now economic rather than military. All of the reform reports used test score data to argue that the nation's schools were failing. (See Stedman and Smith 1983 for an excellent analysis of the 1980s reform reports.) Most of the reports also saw testing as a policy mechanism that would remedy the ills disclosed by testing in the first place. For example, a follow-up study to *A Nation at Risk* found that thirty-five states had enacted testing requirements and forty-four had strengthened graduation requirements (National Commission on Excellence in Education 1983b).

In the late 1980s, John Jacob Cannell found that all states, and the vast majority of school systems, scored above average on standardized achievement tests (dubbed "the Lake Wobegone phenomenon"). This finding called into question the efficacy of the mandated-measurement-driven instruction programs of the '70s and '80s (Cannell 1987, 1988). Cannell's work paved the way for calls in the 1990s for new forms of assessment.

Finally, the reform movement of the 1990s saw a reemphasis of concern over U.S. economic competitiveness and what was perceived to be the poor performance in math and science of our students compared to students in other countries. In response, the President and the nation's governors agreed on six goals for the reform of U.S. education. *America 2000* incorporated those goals and called for the establishment of "world class standards" and a national testing program to monitor progress toward the goals and the attainment of those standards (U.S. Department of Education 1991).

The idea that the United States needs to create a "national" test or testing system has appeal. Advocates argue that the creation of such a test or system is essential if the United States is to develop a world class education system, one that will motivate the unmotivated, lift all students to world class standards, increase our nation's productivity, and restore our global competitiveness. The NCEST was created by Public Law 102-62 on June 27, 1991, to provide Congress with advice on the desirability and feasibility of national standards and testing in education. It can be argued that the feasibility of creating a national testing system was never adequately addressed by NCEST (Koretz, Madaus, Haertel, and Beaton 1992). Nonetheless, the NCEST report argued that "standards and assessments linked to world class standards can become the cornerstone of the fundamental, systemic reform necessary to improve schools" (NCEST 1992, 5). Testing, albeit referred to by the new buzzword "authentic" assessment, was once again touted as the policy tool of choice to hold schools and individuals accountable and reenergize American schools.

We would be remiss if we failed to point out that while testing played an important role in informing educational critics from the 1950s onward, testing itself was also the subject of intense criticism during the same period (see Haney 1981; Haney, Madaus, and Lyons 1993; and Kellaghan, Madaus, and Airasian 1982 for reviews of literature critical of testing from 1950 to 1990). Consider, for example, the following sampling of books critical of the role of testing in our society:

- Martin Gross's *The Brain Watchers* (1962)

- Banish Hoffman's *The Tyranny of Testing* (1962)

- Hillel Black's *They Shall Not Pass* (1963)

- Vance Packard's *The Naked Society* (1964)

- Brian Simon's *Intelligence, Psychology and Education* (1971)

- Leon Kamin's *The Science and Politics of IQ* (1974)

- Joel Spring's *The Sorting Machine* (1976)

- Block and Dworkin's *The IQ Controversy* (1976)

- Paul Houts's *The Myth of Measurability* (1977)

- J. Lawler's *IQ, Heritability, and Racism* (1978)

- Allan Nairn and Associates' *The Reign of ETS: The Corporation That Makes Up Minds* (1980)

- Mitch Lazarus's *Good-bye to Excellence: A Critical Look at the Minimum Competency Testing Movement* (1981)

- George Madaus's *The Courts, Validity, and Minimum Competency Testing* (1982)

- Stephen Jay Gould's *The Mismeasure of Man* (1981)

- Andrew Strenio's *The Testing Trap* (1981)

- David Owen's *None of the Above* (1985)

- James Crouse and Dale Trusheim's *The Case Against the SAT* (1988)

Most of these books dealt with the IQ controversy or the use of the SAT. However, Hoffman (1962) and Houts (1977) remarkably foreshadowed the criticism of multiple-choice testing and the move to alternative assessment techniques that broke through in the 1990s.

The Focus on Outcomes of Schooling

The last fifty years have seen a fundamental shift in the way in which people perceived the quality of schools. Reformers through the early '60s focused on *inputs*, such as the quality of the physical plant, characteristics of teachers, and school finance, as measures of school quality (e.g., Conant 1961). In 1966, the *Equality of Education Opportunity Report* (EEOR), or *Coleman Report*, found that "schools bring little to bear on a child's achievement that is independent of his background and general social context." This widely publicized finding shifted the focus of discussion about equality of opportunity away from inputs to the *outcomes* of schooling (Coleman et al. 1966). (The EEOR's major finding was widely debated, and the data were reanalyzed. For a discussion of that literature, see Madaus, Airasian, and Kellaghan 1980.)

The shift away from school resources toward school outputs measured by tests of academic achievement clearly contributed to the prominence of testing as a policy tool of accountability from the '40s to the present.

Legislation

Whereas state-mandated testing programs contributed to the increase in testing (see fig. 1.1), major pieces of federal legislation enacted between 1957 and 1990 reinforced the upsurge in testing documented in figures 1.2 and 1.3. In addition, myriad federal programs mandated research or evaluation of programs for children; and this evaluation at least indirectly contributed to increased test use. For example, one study identified more than 1,500 test titles proposed for use in federally funded research projects (Heyneman and Mintz 1976).

The following federal education acts were the most prominent (see Haney, Madaus, and Lyons 1993, for a more detailed legislative history):

1. *The National Defense Education Act (NDEA) of 1958*, which included a section entitled "Guidance, Counseling and Testing: Identification and Encouragement of Able Students." That section authorized funds for local testing programs in both public and private school systems. Many of the NDEA's testing provisions were included in the *Elementary and Secondary Education Act of 1965*.

2. *The 1964 Civil Rights Act* made an impact on testing in important ways. For programs and activities receiving federal funding, Title VI mandated non-discrimination in employment by reason of race; and it was widely used to challenge educational testing practices. Two of the most famous of these legal challenges were the *Larry P. v. Riles* case in California, which resulted in the prohibition on the use of IQ tests to place students in classrooms for "educable" mentally retarded students, and the landmark *Debra P. v. Turlington* case in Florida, which ruled that a minimum competency test used for high school graduation had to be a fair test of what was taught in the classrooms of the state (Madaus 1983). The 1964 Civil Rights Act also mandated the *Coleman Report*, which helped to shift the definition of equal opportunity from inputs to educational outcomes, as measured by tests.

3. *The National Assessment of Educational Progress* (NAEP), founded in 1963, marks another milestone in the growing federal influence on educational testing. NAEP, almost entirely funded by the federal government since the late '60s, is important, not because it contributed to increased volume in testing but for several other reasons. First, NAEP was the first systematic effort to gather nationally representative achievement test data. Second, NAEP contributed to the shift to focusing on outcomes when considering educational quality. Third, NAEP data were used to support calls for educational reform in the '70s, '80s, and '90s. (Over the past decade, NAEP's capability to provide accurate information to policymakers and the public stands in sharp contrast to many state and district high-stakes testing programs implemented during the late '70s and '80s in response to a growing dissatisfaction with our schools.) Fourth, NAEP has contributed to the development of curriculum frameworks and to the technology of testing in areas like scaling, matrix sampling, and the reporting of results.

   In 1991, Congress authorized state-by-state comparisons that had initially been prohibited to NAEP. Thirty-five states participated in the effort. (See Glaser and Linn 1992 for an evaluation of the Trial State Assessment Project.) A recommendation by the National Assessment Governing Board (NAGB 1990) and a proposal in the *America 2000* report would extend NAEP downward to district, school, and even individual levels (Haney and Madaus 1992). These later proposals have the potential to change the character of NAEP, perhaps even destroy its usefulness as an independent, valid indicator of the nation's educational progress, and need to be watched closely (Haney and Madaus 1992).

4. *The Elementary and Secondary Education Act* (ESEA) *of 1965* and its subsequent amendments and reauthorizations have had an enormous impact on test use. For example, ESEA provided funds for statewide testing programs and helped upgrade the capacity of state agencies to conduct testing programs. It also provided money under Title IV for the training of personnel conducting tests and measures.

   Standardized test scores became the yardstick to evaluate Title I programs for the disadvantaged and other interventions, such as Head Start [Title II of the Economic Opportunity ACT (ECO) of 1964] and Follow Through (included in a 1967 amendment to the ECO). In 1975, the U.S. Department of Education developed six models for districts to use with either norm- or criterion-referenced tests when evaluating Title I (later Chapter 1 of P.L. 100-297). Section 22 of the 1978 revision included a provision for periodic testing of basic skills achievement and the publication of performance by grade level and school. Because of ESEA, all major achievement-test series were revised in the late '70s and early '80s and included a provision for interpreting results in terms of NCEs. The redesigned achievement series of the late '70s contained a higher density of easier items, making them more useful in the evaluation of programs for the educationally disadvantaged because the change permitted low-achieving students to more reliably show what they knew and could do (Rudman 1987).

5. *The Education for All Handicapped Children Act of 1975* (P.L. 94-142), together with its accompanying regulations and amendments, was another federal windfall for the testing industry. It required that tests and other evaluation materials be used to determine individual placement, assess specific areas of need, and evaluate the effectiveness of individual educational plans of students with disabilities or other special needs (Haney and Madaus 1992).

6. *The Augustus F. Hawkins-Robert T. Stafford Elementary and Secondary School Improvements Amendments of 1988* (P.L. 100-297) contained the first-of-its-kind provisions for a federal test of individual students. It authorized the Secretary of Education

> after consultation with appropriate State and local educational agencies and public and private organizations, to approve comprehensive tests of academic excellence or to develop such a test where commercially unavailable, to be administered to identify outstanding students who are in the eleventh grade of public and private secondary schools . . . . The tests of academic excellence shall be tests of acquired skills and knowledge appropriate for the completion of a secondary school education (P.L. 100-297, 102; STAT. 247-248).

The bill also authorized the Secretary to award certificates to students who scored at a high level. Students would receive these certificates, signed by the Secretary, within 60 days of taking the test.

Bureaucratization of Education

Perhaps the greatest single change in American education over the past fifty years has been the increased bureaucratization of education (see Hall 1977; Wise 1979; and Haney, Madaus, and Lyons 1993 for detailed discussions of testing and bureaucratization). For instance:

- Tests provide means for categorizing people, educational institutions, and problems according to abstract, impersonal, and generalizable rules. They expedite formal and impersonal yet generalizable administrative procedures. Individual test scores can easily be "aggregated" across students to describe the performance of such units as classrooms, schools, school districts, or states.

- Test results have become a standard against which bureaucrats and policymakers can measure the performance of students and educators. Gains or declines in score patterns for aggregated units can then be used as a standard by which to judge the "success" or the "progress" of teachers, administrators, schools, districts, and states toward the realization of certain expectations.

- Tests provide society with a mechanism for the allocation of opportunities on the basis of objective qualifications or merit.

- Testing is an efficient, cheap, administratively convenient, quantifiable, outwardly objective and valid, apparently scientific instrumentality in the service of accountability. Tests provide bureaucrats and policymakers with a convenient mechanism to mete out rewards or sanctions. Affixing important rewards or sanctions to these aggregated mean scores permits bureaucrats and policymakers to put teeth into the accountability system.

- Test scores permit the quantifiable objectification of individuals and of groups. Students' scores on mandated tests easily become part of their permanent records. Students' scores also can be used to make decisions about placement, promotion, or graduation—a form of student-level accountability.

THE FUTURE OF TESTING

Testing will surely remain in the forefront as the policy tool of choice in efforts to reform our educational system. There will be a further push to develop a "voluntary," national , but not federal, testing system along the lines outlined in the NCEST report. Much of the focus on testing as a tool of policy will revolve around "authentic" or "innovative" performance-based assessments. These "new"—actually quite old—forms of assessment have been, and will continue to be, touted as beneficial: as providing real incentives, driving instruction and learning in positive ways, and focusing learning on "higher order or complex thinking skills" (NCEST 1992, 28). Such claims about the efficacy of these assessments need to be carefully evaluated. It is not the form of the tests (e.g., multiple-choice, performance task, portfolio, or product to be evaluated) that is important in determining the impact of a testing program on students, teachers, and schools. Instead it is the use to which the results are put (Messick 1989).

Thus, many issues need careful study before we embark on a new type of national, high-stakes testing program. First, we need to be certain that delivery standards—the necessary inputs and processes that students need to help them meet standards—are in place for all students.

Second, we need more evidence that assessments are preferable to traditional written tests in terms of their effects on the ways teachers and students spend their time and the aspects of the curriculum to which they pay attention. We need to continuously monitor whether a national testing system is narrowing instruction and eventually corrupting the assessments themselves, as happened during the '70s and '80s. New assessment techniques may be more useful to teachers than traditional tests—but how can they be integrated into the normal routines of the classroom? And what happens when we try to use the same techniques simultaneously for making high-stakes decisions about students, teachers, or schools?

Third, the technical issues associated with these assessment techniques will not go away. Evidence is mounting that student performance often generalizes poorly across related performance tasks purporting to measure the same domain or skills. As a result, a student might be judged to fail on the basis of one limited sample of tasks when he would have passed if given equally defensible alternative tasks (Koretz, Madaus, Haertel, and Beaton 1992; Madaus and Kellaghan 1993). Much more research on the validity and fairness of "new" assessment techniques is needed.

Fourth, if we move to a cluster of testing bodies or boards, we need to take seriously the need to have comparable tests across the United States. However, we know from Europe that comparability of performance on exams across diverse examining bodies is very difficult to achieve (Madaus and Kellaghan 1991). Finally, we must address the serious practical problems that occur with new assessments used for high-states policy purposes. Among these problems are manageability; standardization of conditions, which relates to comparability of results even with a single examining body; time constraints; and costs (Koretz, Madaus, Haertel, and Beaton 1992; Madaus 1991; Madaus and Kellaghan 1991, 1993). For example, when England administered the Standard Assessment Tasks (performance tasks) to all seven-year-olds in the springs of 1991, specific issues became apparent: the need for extra support staff in schools, the need for procedures to minimize the disruption of school and classroom organization, and the difficulty (and perhaps undesirability) of imposing standardized conditions of administration that would permit comparability of results across schools. If the English experience taught us anything, it is that there is no quick and easy way of rating large numbers of performance tasks (Madaus and Kellaghan in press).

Testing/assessment, like other technologies, needs to be periodically reevaluated to determine whether it has shifted from being a means used to satisfy a need, to being an end in itself (Staudenmaier 1985). This shift in testing from a means to an end is wonderfully illustrated in the following observation from a 19th century British school inspector who observed firsthand the negative effects of a high-stakes testing program operating in England and Ireland. This program tied pupil examination results to teacher salaries:

> Whenever the outward standard of reality (examination results) has established itself at the expense of the inward, the ease with which worth (or what passes for such) can be measured is ever tending to become in itself the chief, if not sole, measure of worth. And in proportion as we tend to value the results of education for their measurableness, so we tend to undervalue and at last to ignore those results which are too intrinsically valuable to be measured (Holmes 1911, 128).

Sixty years later, Ralph Tyler echoed the same message when he warned that society conspires to treat scores on important certifying tests as the major end of secondary schooling, rather than as useful but not infallible indicator of student achievement (Tyler 1963).

Over ASCD's history, tests have too often been uncritically accepted by far too many people as authoritative and appropriate, without properly evaluating their impact. This is especially true of tests mandated by state law or regulation. The mandate itself lends a legitimacy to a test that is not true of most other technologies. Because testing is so entrenched in our culture, and so taken for granted, most people fail to consider how education is transformed by the mediating role of testing (Madaus 1988). Our hope is that in the coming years, testing and assessment—call it what you may—will be evaluated not only for their contributions to bureaucratic goals of efficiency and productivity, and for their positive and negative side effects, but also for the ways in which they can objectify specific forms of power and authority (Madaus 1990; Messick 1989). Testing and assessment have important roles to play in education; what we need for the remainder of this century—and into the next—are ways to properly evaluate, prioritize, and monitor those roles.

REFERENCES AND FURTHER RESOURCES

Angoff and Dyer. (1971). *The College Board Admissions Testing Program: A Technical Report on Research and Development Activities Relating to the Scholastic Aptitude Test and Achievement Tests.* New York: College Entrance Examinations Board.

Aries, P. (1962). *Centuries of Childhood: A Social History of Family Life.* New York: Vintage Books.

Basalla, G. (1988). *The Evolution of Technology.* New York: Cambridge University Press.

Black, H. (1963). *They Shall Not Pass.* New York: Morrow.

Block, N. J., and G. Dworkin. (1976). *The IQ Controversy.* New York: Pantheon Books.

Bloom, B. S. (1968). "Learning for Mastery." *University of California Comment* 1, 2: 1-12.

Boorstin, D. J. (1978). *The Republic of Technology: Reflections on Our Future Community.* New York: Harper and Row.

Bowker Annual. (1970-1987). New York: R. R. Bowker.

Bowler, R. F. (1983). "Payment by Results: A Study in Achievement Accountability." Doctoral diss., Boston College.

Bruner, J. S. (1966). *Toward a Theory of Instruction.* Cambridge, MA: Belknap Press of Harvard University Press.

Buros, O. C. (1938). *Nineteen Thirty-Eight Mental Measurements Yearbook of the School of Education.* New Brunswick, NJ: Rutgers University Press.

Burton, E. (1979). "Richard Lowell Edgeworth's Education Bill of 1979: A Missing Chapter in the History of Irish Education." *Irish Journal of Education* 13, 1:24-33.

Cannell, J. J. (1987). *Nationally Normed Elementary Achievement Testing in America's Public Schools: How All Fifty States Are Above the National Average.* Daneils, WV: Friends for Education.

————. (1988). "Nationally Normed Elementary Achievement Testing in America's Public Schools: How All Fifty States Are Above the National Average." *Educational Measurement: Issues and Practice* 7, 2: 5-9.

Carroll, J. (1963). "A Model for School Learning." *Teachers College Record* 64: 723-733.

Carroll, J. B. (1987). "The National Assessments in Reading: Are We Misreading the Findings?" *Phi Delta Kappan* 68, 6: 424-430.

Coleman, J. S., E. Q. Campbell, C. J. Hobson, J. McPartland, A. M. Mood, F. D. Weinfield, and R. L. York. (1966). *Equality of Educational Opportunity.* Washington, DC: Office of Education, U.S. Department of Health, Education, and Welfare, U.S. Government Printing Office.

Conant, J. B. (1961). *Slums and Suburbs: A Commentary on Schools in Metropolitan Areas.* New York: McGraw-Hill.

Conoley, J. C. and J. J. Kramer, eds. (1989). *Tenth Mental Measurements Yearbook*. Lincoln, NE: Buros Institute of Mental Measurements of the University of Nebraska-Lincoln.

Coolahan, J. M. (1975). "The Origins of the Payment-by-Results Policy in Education and the Experience of It in the National and Intermediate Schools of Ireland." Master's thesis, Trinity College, Dublin.

Crouse, J., and D. Trusheim. (1988). *The Case Against the SAT*. Chicago: University of Chicago Press.

Edmonds, R. R. (1980). "Schools Count: New York City's School Improvement Project." *Harvard Graduate School of Education Association Bulletin* 25: 33-35.

Ellul, J. (1990). *The Technological Bluff*. Grand Rapids, MI: Williams B. Eerdmans.

Foucault, M. (1977). *Discipline and Punish. The Birth of the Prison*. New York: Viking.

Glaser, R., and R. Linn. (1992). "Assessing Student Achievement in the States." The first report of the National Academy of Education Panel on the Evaluation of the NAEP Trial State Assessments: *1990 Trial State Assessment*. Stanford, CA: National Academy of Education.

Gordon, S. C. (1968). *Reports and Repercussions in West Indian Education. 1835-1933*. London: Ginn.

Gould, S. J. (1981). *The Mismeasure of Man*. New York: Norton.

Gross, M. L. (1962). *The Brain Watchers*. New York: Random House.

Haertel, E. (1989). "Student Achievement Tests as Tools of Educational Policy: Practices and Consequences." In *Test Policy and Test Performance: Education, Language and Culture*, edited by B. Gifford. Boston: Kluwer Academic Publishers.

Hall, E. T. (1976). *Beyond Culture*. Garden City, NY: Anchor Press.

Haney, W., and G. F. Madaus. (1992). "Cautions on Removing the Prohibition Against the Use of NAEP Tests and Data Reporting Below the State Level." In *Studies for the Evaluation of the National Assessment of Educational Progress (NAEP) Trial State Assessment*. Stanford, CA: National Academy of Education.

Haney, W., G. F. Madaus, and R. Lyons. (1993). *The Fractured Marketplace of Standardized Testing*. Boston: Kluwer Academic Publishers.

Hearn, W. E. (1872). *Payment by the Results in Primary Education*. Melbourne: Stellwell and Knight.

Herrnstein, R. (September 1971). "IQ." *Atlantic Monthly*, 63-64.

Heyneman, S. P., and P. Mintz. (1976). *The Frequency and Quality of Measures Utilized in Federally Sponsored Research on Children*. Washington, DC: Social Research Group, George Washington University.

Hoffman, B. (1962). *The Tyranny of Testing*. New York: Crowell-Collier Press.

Holmes, E. G. A. (1911). *What Is and What Might Be: A Study of Education in General and Elementary in Particular.* London: Constable.

Hoskins, K. (1968). "The Examination, Disciplinary Power and Rational Schooling." *History of Education* 8: 135-146.

Houts, P. (1977). *The Myth of Measurability.* New York: Hart.

Hughes, R. N. (March 15, 1979). "Education Could Pay." *New York Times,* A23.

Hughes, T. P. (1989). *American Genesis: A Century of Invention and Technological Enthusiasm.* New York: Penguin Books.

Jensen, A. (1969). "How Much Can We Boost IQ and Scholastic Achievement?" *Harvard Educational Review* 33: 1-123.

Judd, C. H. (1918). "A Look Forward." In *The Measurement of Educational Products,* edited by G. M. Whipple. Bloomington, IL: Public School Publishing Co.

Kamin, L. J. (1974). *The Science and Politics of I.Q.* Potomac, MD: Lawrence Erlbaum Associates.

Kellaghan, T., G. F. Madaus, and P. W. Airasian. (1982). *The Effects of Standardized Testing.* Boston: Kluwer-Nijhoff.

Keppel, F. (1966). *The Necessary Revolution in American Education.* (1st ed.). New York: Harper and Row.

Koretz, D. M., G. F. Madaus, E. Haertel, and A. Beaton. (February 19, 1992). Statement before the Subcommittee on Elementary, Secondary, and Vocational Education Committee on Education and Labor, U.S. House of Representatives, Washington, D.C.

Laffer, A. B. (1982). "For Better Schools, Pay Achievers." *Education Week* 24: 25.

Lawler, J. M. (1978). *IQ, Heritability, and Racism.* New York: International Publishers.

Lazarus, M. (1981). *Goodbye to Excellence: A Critical Look at Minimum Competency Testing.* Boulder, CO: Westview Press.

Levine, D. M. (1971). *Performance Contracting in Education. An Appraisal: Toward a Balanced Perspective.* Englewood Cliffs, NJ: Educational Technology Publications.

Lowrance, W. W. (1986). *Modern Science and Human Values.* New York: Oxford University Press.

Madaus, G. F. (1983 ed.). *The Courts, Validity, and Minimum Competency Testing.* Boston: Kluwer-Nijhoff.

———. (1985). "Public Policy and the Testing Profession—You've Never Had It So Good?" *Educational Measurement: Issues and Practices* 4, 4: 5-11.

———. (1988). "The Influence of Testing on the Curriculum." In *Critical Issues in Curriculum,* edited by L. Tanner. Chicago: University of Chicago Press.

————. (1990). "Testing as a Social Technology: The Inaugural Boisi Lecture in Education and Public Policy." Center for the Study of Testing, Evaluation, and Public Policy, Boston College.

————. (1991). "The Effects of Important Tests on Students: Implications for a National Examination or System of Examinations." *Phi Delta Kappan* 73, 3: 226-231.

Madaus, G. F., P. W. Airasian, and T. Kellaghan. (1980). *School Effectiveness: A Reassessment of the Evidence*. New York: McGraw-Hill.

Madaus, G. F., and T. Kellaghan. (1991). *Student Examination Systems in the European Community: Lessons for the United States*. Contractor Report submitted to the Office of Technology Assessment, U.S. Congress, Washington, D.C.

————. (1992). "Curriculum Evaluation and Assessment." In *Handbook of Research on Curriculum*, edited by P. W. Jackson. New York: Macmillan.

————. (February 1993). "British Experience with 'Authentic' Testing." *Phi Delta Kappan* 74, no. 6: 458-469.

Madaus, G. F., and J. T. McDonagh. (1979). "Minimum Competency Testing: Unexamined Assumptions and Unexplored Negative Outcomes." *New Directions for Testing and Measurement* 3:1-15.

Marx, L. (1988). *The Pilot and the Passenger: Essays on Literature, Technology, and Culture in the United States*. New York: Oxford University Press.

Massachusetts Historical Society Documents. (1845-1846). "Horace Mann Papers." Microfilm Collection 372, Reel 8 (August 29, 1845).

Messick, S. (1989). "Validity." In *Educational Measurement*, edited by R. Linn. 3rd ed. New York: Macmillan.

Montgomery, R. J. (1967) *Examinations: An Account of Their Evolution as Administrative Devices in England*. Pittsburgh: University of Pittsburgh Press.

Nairn, A., and Associates. (1980). *The Reign of ETS: The Corporation That Makes Up Minds*. The Ralph Nader Report on the Educational Testing Service. Washington, DC: Ralph Nader.

National Commission on Excellence in Education. (1983a). *A Nation at Risk*. Washington, DC: U.S. Government Printing Office.

————. (1983b). *Meeting the Challenge: Recent Efforts to Improve Education Across the Nation*. Washington, DC: U.S. Government Printing Office.

National Commission on Testing and Public Policy (NCTPP). (1990). *From Gatekeeper to Gateway: Transforming Testing in America*. Chestnut Hill, MA: NCTPP, Boston College.

National Council on Education Standards and Testing (NCEST). (1992). *Raising Standards for American Education: A Report to Congress, the Secretary of Education, the National Education Goals Panel, and the American People*. Washington, DC: NCEST.

Owen, D. (1985). *None of the Above: Behind the Myth of Scholastic Aptitude*. Boston: Houghton-Mifflin.

Pacey, A. (1989). *The Culture of Technology*. Cambridge, MA: Massachusetts Institute of Technology Press.

Packard, V. O. (1964). *The Naked Society*. New York: D. McKay.

Popham, W. J. (1983). "Measurements as an Instructional Catalyst." *New Directions for Testing and Measurement* 17:19-20.

Romberg, T. A., E. A. Zarinnia, and S. R. Williams. (1989). *The Influence of Mandated Testing on Mathematics Instruction: Grade 8 Teachers' Perceptions*. Madison, WI: University of Wisconsin, National Center for Research in Mathematical Science Education.

Rosenthal, R., and L. Jacobson. (1968). *Pygmalion in the Classroom*. New York: Holt, Rinehart and Winston.

Rudman, H. C. (1987). "The Future of Testing Is Now." *Educational Measurement: Issues and Practice* 6:5-11.

Samelson, F. (1987). "Was Early Mental Testing: (a) Racist Inspired, (b) Objective Science, (c) A Technology for Democracy, (d) The Origin of Multiple-choice Exams, (e) None of the Above?" In *Psychological Testing and American Society: 1890-1930*, edited by M. M. Sokal. New Brunswick, NJ: Rutgers University Press.

Shanker, A. (October 26, 1986). "Power v. Knowledge in St. Louis: Professionalism Under Fire." *New York Times*, E7.

Simon, B. (1971). *Intelligence, Psychology, and Education: A Marxist Critique*. London: Lawrence and Wishart.

Snow, R., and E. Yalow. (1982). "Education and Intelligence." In *Handbook of Human Intelligence*, edited by R. J. Sternberg. Cambridge, England: Cambridge University Press.

Sokal, M. M., ed. (1987). *Psychological Testing and American Society: 1890-1930*. New Brunswick, NJ: Rutgers University Press.

Spring, J. H. (1976). *The Sorting Machine: A National Educational Policy Since 1945*. New York: McKay.

Starch and Elliott. (1912). "Reliability of Grading High School Work in English." *School Review* 21: 442-457.

———. (1913). "Reliability of Grading Work in Mathematics." *School Review* 21: 254-259.

Staudenmaier, J. M. (1985). *Technology's Storytellers: Reweaving the Human Fabric*. Cambridge, MA: Massachusetts Institute of Technology Press.

———. (1989). "U.S. Technological Style and the Atrophy of Civic Commitment." In *Beyond Individualism Toward a Retrieval of Moral Discourse in America*, edited by D. L. Gilpi. South Bend, IN: Notre Dame Press.

Stedman, L. C., and M. S. Smith. (1983). "Recent Reform Proposals for American Education." *Contemporary Education Review* 2, 2: 85-104.

Strenio, J. A. (1981). *The Testing Trap: How It Can Make or Break Your Career and Your Children's Futures*. New York: Rawson, Wade Publishers.

Sutherland, G. (1973). *Elementary Education in the Nineteenth Century*. London: London Historical Association.

Thorndike, R. M., and D. F. Lohman. (1990). *A Century of Ability Testing*. Chicago: Riverside.

Travers, R. M. W. (1983). *How Research Has Changed American Schools: A History from 1840 to the Present*. Kalamazoo, MI: Mythos Press.

Tyack, D. B. (1974). *The One Best System: A History of American Urban Education*. Cambridge, MA: Harvard University Press.

Tyack, D., and E. Hansot. (1982). *Managers of Virtue: Public School Leadership in America*. New York: Basic Books.

Tyler, R. W. (1963). "The Impact of External Testing Programs." In *The Impact and Improvement of School Testing Programs*, edited by W. G. Findley. Chicago: University of Chicago Press.

U.S. Department of Education. (1991). *America 2000: An Education Strategy: Sourcebook*. (ED/OS91-13). Washington, DC: U.S. Department of Education.

White, E. E. (1888). "Examinations and Promotions." *Education* 8:519-522.

Winner. L. (1977). *Autonomous Technology: Technics-Out-of-Control as a Theme in Political Thought*. Cambridge, MA: Massachusetts Institute of Technology Press.

―――. (1986). *The Whale and the Reactor: A Search for Limits in an Age of High Technology*. Chicago: University of Chicago Press.

Wise, A. E. (1979). *Legislated Learning: The Bureaucratization of the American Classroom*. Berkeley: University of California Press.

Woody, C., and P. V. Sangren. (1933). *Administration of the Testing Program*. New York: World Book Co.

2

Library Information Skills and Standardized Achievement Tests

 MARY M. JACKSON

LIBRARY SKILLS/INFORMATION SKILLS—A PARADIGM SHIFT

During the past decade, library skills have been evolving from primarily information location skills to information-processing skills (Eisenberg and Berkowitz 1988; Irving 1985; Kuhlthau 1985; Stripling and Pitts 1988). "The [new] emphasis is on developing transferable cognitive skills that should increase students' effective use of information in general as well as their use of specific libraries and resources" (Eisenberg 1992). Eisenberg also stipulates that "specific library and information skills should be taught within the context of an overall process" (1992). Specific cognitive skills mentioned in the works previously cited include, but are not limited to, identifying the problem and the topic or information needed; locating the information; analyzing or interpreting the information; synthesizing and organizing the information; using the information; and evaluating, either in terms of the quality, suitability, or relevance of the information for a specific need or in terms of the search process.

Those familiar with the *Taxonomy of Cognitive Objectives* (Bloom 1956) will note the similarities between Bloom's taxonomy and the information-search process, not just in the use of certain terminology but in how students work with or should work with information. These skills are also described as "critical thinking" skills, meaning that students need to be able to do more than simply recall information (Ennis 1962).

Bloom characterized the cognitive skills of comprehension, application, analysis, synthesis, and evaluation of information as being of a "higher order," more complicated than the cognitive skill of recall. Although Bloom's committee classified and described these theoretical cognitive, or thinking, skills to facilitate communication among psychologists and educators, evidence of how they function is more difficult to determine (Mueller 1991). Recall, however, is much easier to assess and, in fact, has been the cognitive skill most frequently called upon when students take examinations. For example, test questions frequently require recollection of lecture notes or textbook material.

Reprinted from *School Library Media Annual, 1993* (pp. 22-29) by Carol Collier Kuhlthau, ed. Englewood, CO: Libraries Unlimited. Copyright 1993. Used with permission.

If higher-order skills are also the basic skills needed in the information research process, then they should be the skills taught and practiced in the "information skills curriculum." The importance of these skills is also being reinforced by labor and business leaders who are calling for a new work force educated in these skills (Secretary's Commission on Achieving Necessary Skills 1992; Task Force on Education for Economic Growth 1983).

TRADITIONAL LIBRARY
LOCATION SKILLS

Within the "information location" stage of the information-search process can be found the more traditional library search skills upon which library instruction was founded. Location skills have long been the keystone of library instruction and testing efforts. These traditional location skills taught in schools were summarized 60 years ago in Fargo's *Library in the School* (1933). Many of the subsequent attempts (Farris 1986; Henslowe 1978; Humphry 1954; Rossoff 1961; Sitter 1982) to define and delimit the scope of library skills needed by students basically repeat Fargo's work. Occasionally very brief mention was made of keyword identification, skimming, outlining, note-taking, precis writing, footnoting, and bibliography writing. Farris (1986) was the only author to mention computer skills as necessary, and these were limited to word-processing and database compilation skills, not information retrieval skills. These early location skills were frequently found in scope and sequence charts used in schools around the country. The recall of specific library location tools usually formed the basis of assessment for these skills.

Ten years after Bloom's *Taxonomy* was compiled, Henne (1966) concluded that being able to locate information was of little intellectual benefit to students. She stated that what students *did* with information—namely, evaluating, comprehending, analyzing, synthesizing, and using—was much more important. Henne's identification of these skills marks the beginning of the development of the information skills curriculum.

ASSESSMENT OF LIBRARY INFORMATION
SKILLS ON STANDARDIZED
ACHIEVEMENT TESTS

Linked to the drive for academic excellence within our schools and the public's insistence on accountability, assessment of academic achievement is of great interest to society. Standardized achievement testing is one method of examining academic accomplishments, although the results of these tests are often given too much emphasis for the wrong reasons (Woolls 1991). The inclusion of library and study skills questions on standardized achievement tests indicates, however, that these skills are important parts of the nation's curricula. A review of the characteristics of standardized achievement tests might help to clarify their use in the assessment of library information skills.

Standardized achievement tests are carefully written and evaluated before being released for use by schools. The standardization process ensures their reliability, which means that they produce consistent results when used across several normative groups. Defined procedures for administration lessen effects of intervening variables such as space, time, and climate. Because these tests are expensive to produce, however, there are only a few companies that can underwrite their development. To survive, these companies must show profit for their investment. This means they must make their tests as acceptable as possible to the widest school market. Also, the contents of these tests are generally based on the contents of current textbooks and curriculum guides in common use across the nation at the time the tests are written. Unfortunately, textbooks and curriculum guides as well as standardized achievement tests have writing and publishing time lags. These tests would, therefore, possibly *not* reflect the most current research and thinking on a topic. Thus, controversial or recently defined skills or process questions might be difficult to find on current standardized achievement tests.

Standardized achievement tests have generally relied on multiple-choice test items to facilitate speed and ease of scoring. Good test items are difficult to write; questions that require recall of factual information or application of test-given information would most likely be easier to compose. There is even some confusion about whether the cognitive skills of analysis, synthesis, or evaluation can be assessed via multiple-choice test items. For instance, Norris (1989) concludes that multiple-choice test items are not suited to assessing cognitive thought processes. He indicates that generalizations about thought processes have not been formulated in such a way that thought processes might be assessed on tests. In other words, Norris suggests that multiple-choice tests do not provide evidence of definite thought processes and would be poor choices to determine skills of analysis, synthesis, and evaluation.

It can also be difficult to determine the specific type of higher-order thinking skill required to answer library skills questions on standardized achievement tests. Lien reports that

> sometimes teachers . . . have difficulty agreeing upon the [thinking skill] category into which a given question fits. At times, teachers believe that a certain type of question will elicit the same kind of thinking among all the pupils. For example, if a teacher wanted students to determine which era in the literature was best portrayed by quotations, for some students it would require interpretation. However, for those who may remember the quotation by a certain author and era, it would be exhibiting only memory. (Lien 1980, 87)

For the purpose of this chapter, library and study skills sections of three standardized achievement tests were examined to attempt to determine whether answering the questions on these tests requires only the cognitive skill of memory or whether higher-order cognitive skills may also be involved. The subject matter of each of the three tests was also noted.

The three tests reviewed are the Iowa Test of Educational Development (ITED), 1989; the Tests of Achievement and Proficiency (TAP), 1990; and the Comprehensive Tests of Basic Skills, fourth edition (CTBS4), 1989. In each case, the highest level for high school students was examined. The quoted information included in the following is from manuals and brochures that accompany these tests.

The Iowa Test of Educational Development

46 total questions

Subtest title: "Use of Sources of Information"

Stated purpose: "to evaluate the student's ability to utilize important sources of information." Students will understand "how to use libraries, reference books, and other sources of information." They will select "appropriate sources to find needed information."

Subject matter: Books including organization and use of parts, dictionaries, organization of library materials, encyclopedias, almanacs, common references including abstracts and periodicals, *Readers' Guide*, maps, atlases, government and private agencies.

Stated cognitive skills tested: Test questions are classified into two types:

1. Knowledge of the mechanics of using various resources. Requires test-taker "to identify kinds of material included in various types of references; to define the meaning of symbols and abbreviations commonly used in standard reference works; to demonstrate understanding of the way in which material is organized within a source; to identify appropriate use of the parts of a book or reference work; to demonstrate familiarity with the contents and purposes, and to identify examples of appropriate use of various references and sources." This section relies heavily on recall or knowledge of previously learned information.

2. Evaluation skills in judging the suitability of sources for various purposes. Requires test-taker "to select the best or more likely source of information on a given problem." Although this is called evaluation, other skills might be called into use:

   • *identification of problem or information need*—problems stated in paragraph form, require test-takers to isolate specific information before selecting an appropriate answer;

   • *recall*—test-takers must remember specific sources and their characteristics and uses; and

   • *analysis*—test-taker must analyze the characteristic and uses of a specific title from the words in that title to determine its use.

An example would be if the question asked for the best source for a line of poetry and the choices included specific titles of the following: biographical dictionary, a poetry index, a play index, or a thesaurus. Of course, all questions require the skill of "comprehension." Students must understand questions before they can answer them.

Question format: Mostly statements with four possible responses. Both specific reference titles and descriptive words or phrases are used as distractors (choices). Examples are "an almanac," "a gazetteer," "an unabridged dictionary." Questions are also asked about specific examples of library location tools: for example, a catalog card and entries from the *Readers' Guide*.

The Tests of Achievement and Proficiency

68 total questions

Subtest title: "Using Sources of Information"

Stated purpose: "The purpose of this test is to find out how well [students] can use common sources of information, such as charts, maps, graphs, and dictionaries."

Subject matter: Reading a table, a map, a diagram, a graph, a brochure, a table of contents, identifying information need and appropriate source to fulfill need, identifying the parts of dictionary entries and indexes, interpreting information from a merchandise catalog.

Stated cognitive skills tested: Comparison, drawing conclusions and inferences, application, interpretation; also, in a separate chart, each individual question is assigned to one of the following skill categories: knowledge/information (presumably recall or memory), 6 questions; comprehension, 22 questions; application/analysis, 24 questions; and synthesis/evaluation, 16 questions.

Question format: Sixty-one of the 68 questions are based on some type of illustrated information such as chart, graph, page from dictionary, advertisement; this ensures that each student starts from the same information base before answering questions. Many of these 61 questions require comprehension of the presented information as well as analysis of this information before questions can be answered. The dictionary exercise does not require identification of specific abbreviations; 7 questions request identification of where to find answers to specific reference questions; for each of these 7 questions, the same four choices are used and these are basic reference books and the card catalog. Students must analyze characteristics of these four choices to determine which would best fit the information need given.

The Comprehensive Test of Basic Skills

20 total questions

Subtest title: "Study Skills"

Stated purpose: "This test measures a student's ability to find and use information."

Subject matter: Item content is related to "parts of books, dictionary conventions, library skills, reference sources, graphic information . . ."

Stated cognitive skills tested: Organizing and analyzing information. Although the stated cognitive skills are limited to two, the question format requires synthesis and use of information as well. For instance, test-takers are requested to select appropriate notes from a given passage for inclusion in research notes (note-taking) and to select appropriate sentences to fill in blank lines of a given outline. Students are also requested to identify specific titles to fit information needs. Few of the titles are common titles, which indicates that students would need to analyze the words in the specific titles to match their given information need.

Question format: Some questions are asked about given examples of catalog cards, a chart, and an outline. All items are statements with four multiple-choice responses.

SUMMARY AND CONCLUSIONS

Do library and study skills sections of standardized achievement tests measure currently defined library information skills? Are there opportunities for students to identify information problems or needs? Do students have opportunities to evaluate use of potential sources for a given need? Are there opportunities for students to select appropriate information for a given need or analyze information? May they synthesize or use information to draw conclusions, complete outlines, or take notes? Are there opportunities for students to demonstrate information location skills and knowledge? The answers to all of these questions is a qualified yes. Given the format of the examined tests, each showed some effort to assess student knowledge or recall of library information location skills as well as some effort to assess students' skills at demonstrating other information-processing skills such as comprehension, application, analysis, interpretation, synthesis, and evaluation.

What can standardized achievement tests not assess? First, these tests reduce the information process to short questions and answers. Readers of Kuhlthau (1985) will realize that the information search process is a complex process involving thoughts, feelings, and attitudes. Different students will use different cognitive skills when answering the same question. Standardized achievement tests cannot fully assess student mental processes engaged in information use.

Due to their limited space in a complete battery of standardized achievement tests, library-study skills sections can cover only limited subject matter. The entire range and scope of the information search process cannot be covered. Also, test-takers might not ascribe much importance to library-study skills tests because a semester- or year-long class in this subject rarely exists at the high school level. Also, these tests cannot assess feelings and attitudes that might influence the information research process.

Specifically, none of the tests attempted to assess the process of narrowing or broadening a topic. Computerized information retrieval was not addressed on any of the tests. Development of thesis or purpose statements was also not included on any of the tests. None of the test questions covered development of a search strategy, although Hyland's earlier standardized Ohio School Library/Media Test (1978) did include such a question. Interestingly enough, Hyland's normative groups performed poorly on ordering the steps in a search strategy, and she concluded that they had probably not had enough experience in doing so.

In conclusion, results from library-study skills sections of standardized achievement tests provide only limited evidence of successful use of information. Other means of assessment such as portfolio compilations of student work, oral recitations, and professional judgment might be more appropriate for measuring successful information use. The information use process is a complex undertaking with success and failure dependent on many factors other than success or failure on standardized tests. Teachers and school library media specialists as well as school administrators must look for other ways to determine whether their students are ready to take their places in the information-rich society of today.

REFERENCES

Bloom, B. S. *Taxonomy of Educational Objectives: Handbook 1: Cognitive Domain.* New York: David McKay, 1956.

Eisenberg, M. B., and R. E. Berkowitz. *Curriculum Initiative: An Agenda and Strategy for Library Media Programs.* Norwood, NJ: Ablex, 1988.

Eisenberg, M. B., and M. K. Brown. "Current Themes Regarding Library and Information Skills Instruction: Research Supporting and Research Lacking." *School Library Media Quarterly* 20, no. 2 (1992): 103-11.

Ennis, R. H. "A Critical Concept of Critical Thinking." *Harvard Review* 32, no. 1 (1962): 81-111.

Fargo, L. *The Library in the School.* Chicago: American Library Association, 1933.

Farris, M. E. "A Study to Identify and Develop a Library Media Skills Curriculum in Elementary Grades K-6." (Ph.D. diss., Memphis State University, 1986). *Dissertation Abstracts International* 47 (1986): 2002A.

Henne, F. "Learning to Learn in School Libraries." In *The School Library Media Program: Instructional Force for Excellence*, edited by R. A. Davies, 548-55. New York: R. R. Bowker, 1966.

Henslowe, S. A. "Development and Validation of a Library Locational Skills Model for Elementary School Library, Reading, and Social Studies Education." Unpublished Ph.D. diss., University of British Columbia, 1978.

Humphry, B. "The Development of Work-Study Skills in Selected Elementary School Textbooks." Unpublished Ph.D. diss., University of Iowa, 1954.

Hyland, A. M. "Development and Administration of 'The Ohio School Library/Media Test': An Instrument for Assessing a Student's Library/Media Ability." (Ph.D. diss., University of Toledo, 1978). *Dissertation Abstracts International* 7824522 (1978).

Irving, A. *Study and Information Skills Across the Curriculum.* Portsmouth, NH: Heinemann, 1985.

Kuhlthau, C. C. *Teaching the Library Research Process*. West Nyack, NY: Center for Applied Research in Education, 1985.

Lien, A. J. *Measurement and Evaluation of Learning*. 4th ed. Dubuque, IA: William C. Brown, 1980.

Mueller, D. *E-Mail on Cognitive Skills*. Bloomington, IN: Indiana University, 1991.

Norris, S. P. "Can We Test Validly for Critical Thinking?" *Educational Researcher* 18 (1989): 21-26.

Rossoff, M. *The Library in High School Teaching*. 2d ed. New York: H. W. Wilson, 1961.

Secretary's Commission on Achieving Necessary Skills. *Learning a Living: A Blueprint for High Performance*. Washington, DC: U.S. Department of Labor, 1992.

Sitter, C. L. "The Status of and the Need for the Teaching of Library Media and Information Skills in Public Schools of the State of Colorado." (Ph.D. diss., University of Colorado, 1982). *Dissertation Abstracts International* 43 (1982): 3743A.

Stripling, B. K., and J. M. Pitts. *Brainstorms and Blueprints: Teaching Library Research as a Thinking Process*. Englewood, CO: Libraries Unlimited, 1988.

Task Force on Education for Economic Growth. *Action for Excellence—A Comprehensive Plan to Improve Our Nation's Schools*. Denver, CO: Education Commission of the States, 1983.

Woolls, B. "Testing of Information Skills." In *Information Literacy—Papers of the Treasure Mountain Research Retreat #2*, Atlanta, Georgia, 1991. (Contact Hi Willow Research and Publishing, P.O. Box 266, Castle Rock, CO 80104.)

TEST BIBLIOGRAPHY

Comprehensive Test of Basic Skills. 4th ed. Monterey, CA: CTB/McGraw-Hill, 1989.

Iowa Test of Educational Development. Chicago: Riverside, 1988.

Tests of Achievement and Proficiency. Chicago: Riverside, 1990.

3

From Indicators of Quantity to Measures of Effectiveness
Ensuring *Information Power*'s Mission

 ROBERT E. BERKOWITZ

"The mission of the library media program is to ensure that students and staff are effective users of ideas and information."[1] School library media specialists in every corner of our nation have begun to act on this mission statement. At the same time, school district administrators are in the process of assessing instructional programs and justifying the allocation of resources to library media programs. Library media specialists know, by intuition if not validation, that they make a clear and valuable impact on student learning and that their contribution enhances the overall performance goals of the school and school district. If library media specialists are to fulfill their mission, they must convince those who make decisions regarding resources that this is so. Some of the critical information that will influence future decisionmaking is that students

- are competent to enter the information age,

- achieve at higher levels because there is a library media specialist in the school, and

- achieve at higher levels because of a quality library media program.

THE CONTEXT

The responsibility of a school administrator at either the district or building level is to manage the school in such a way as to promote the educational goals. This is accomplished by prioritizing the allocation of resources to those programs that are the most effective in terms of student outcomes and that address strong community concerns. Another key to the distribution of limited resources is whether the program has value—that is, the degree to which the program's impact on the district goals is positive, describable, and visible. Library media specialists, along with the rest of the faculty, must justify their budgets. However, unlike many of their colleagues, library media specialists must also justify their existence within the school. Most of the faculty have state-mandated positions as well as curricular

Reprinted from *School Library Media Annual, 1993* (pp. 3-12) by Carol Collier Kuhlthau, ed. Englewood, CO: Libraries Unlimited. Copyright 1993. Used with permission.

programs. Many school library media specialists, especially in elementary schools, owe their positions to the community's decision that libraries are important to student learning. Even though library media specialists are consulted about administrative decisions regarding library programs and resources (e.g., purchasing new information technologies, introducing flexible scheduling, maintaining full-time professional positions), the reality is that absent persuasive evidence that libraries are essential to learning, such decisions may be based on stereotypes, perceptions, or whim.

Across the country, the call to make school communities accountable for improved learner outcomes has met with programmatic response. Education decisionmakers look for and react positively to information that helps determine the worth of instructional programs. Generally, program effectiveness is embodied in test scores that substantiate curriculum-related achievement (i.e., student performance) and that can be compared to regional, state, and national results. The powers that can be persuaded to listen to the rationale for promoting library media programs and, more important, to actively support them when library media specialists

1. acknowledge faculty/administration/community concerns or criticisms in a straightforward manner;

2. speak to concerns or criticisms in terms and ways educational decisionmakers understand;

3. educate those in power about library media specialists' roles and responsibilities within the framework of *Information Power*; and

4. provide proof that library media specialists have a strong, positive impact in schools.

Ultimately, school authorities are concerned with how much and how well students learn. The focus is on the importance of students being able to competently read, write, and compute. Library media programs play integral roles in accomplishing these learner outcomes. Ideally, in their roles as information specialists, teachers, and instructional consultants, library media specialists provide library and information skills instruction taught within an integrated or unified view of curriculum (i.e., a systematic, sequential, and continually progressive approach to instruction). Additionally, they provide other curriculum-related services such as reading guidance, resources provision, and curriculum development. The library media specialist's effectiveness should and can be made credible in the context of the administrator's focus.

Administrators measure student performance by comparing expectations to actual learner outcomes. They respond positively to formal indicators of how much and how well students are learning content. This content focus is the subject of a variety of assessment techniques such as standardized tests, criterion reference tests, objectives reference tests and, more recently, portfolio assessments. Additionally, administrators are also predisposed to support staff members who work cooperatively and collaboratively. When library media specialists promote and engage in efforts to work with teachers to meet common goals, administrators take notice, especially when such efforts have positive effects on school goals via learner outcomes.

The educational community's recent and growing interest in learner outcomes and performance-based assessment is changing the educational environment and, consequently, how schools will be held accountable for student learning. With the rising interest in learner outcomes and performance-based assessment, new opportunities for library media specialists to assess their impact on students are available. Accepting the challenge of such opportunities can provide the means for program validation.

In schools, each instructional content area has a common framework of policies, goals, and objectives that provide the basis for instruction. The result of applying this framework is curriculum coverage. The degree to which the curriculum is learned is in direct relation to the resources provided, how those resources are organized, and how information is presented to students. School library media specialists link resources, content areas, and information problem-solving processes. Therefore, library media specialists are vital to the quality of instructional programs.

THE FOUNDATION

Library media specialists' responses to administrators' needs for objective information concerning library media programs is already part of the discourse within the library media professional community. Many states, including New York[2] and Maryland,[3] are well under way in designing and implementing learner-outcome-based syllabi for library media programs. In these and many other states, school districts are restructuring their library media curricula to reflect this new focus on learner outcomes. Many educators, including Kuhlthau,[4] Stripling and Pitts,[5] Irving,[6] and Eisenberg and Berkowitz,[7] have presented information problem-solving-process approaches to library and information skills instruction. Library media specialists have the unique perspective that effective instruction involves solving a series of information-based problems. From that posture, process becomes the content of library media instructional programs. The potential impact of teaching information skills on student performance is enormous. Process-oriented education is at the heart of satisfactory learner outcomes. Process and content objectives combine to create performance-based objectives, which in turn can be adjusted in light of learner outcomes.

Establishing performance objectives based on learner outcomes is an important step forward. By establishing criteria for achievement and assessing learner outcomes, library media specialists will have qualitative information that can become the basis for continued program evaluation, growth, and development and for communication to education's decisionmakers regarding the impact of library media programs on student performance.

Included within the guidelines put forward in *Information Power* are sample evaluative criteria:[8]

- the total school population (students and staff) being served

- identified subgroups served; in what ways; with what frequency

- frequency and effectiveness of the library media specialist's participation in instructional planning with teachers

- effectiveness of students in using information resources to meet specific learning objectives

- frequency and effectiveness of teachers using library media resources and activities to accomplish classroom objectives

- library media program's objectives met

The profession's mission statement and its call for changing the guidelines for the assessment of library media programs has not produced the needed results. Traditionally, library media specialists report information such as collection size, new acquisitions, student attendance, total classes taught, and the number of unfulfilled information requests, in either estimated or actual figures. These indicators of quantity seem not to matter to school administrators and boards of education. Certainly, they seem not to have made a positive impact on resource allocation, staffing, and the role of library media professionals in the school. Many of our colleagues are losing their jobs.

As professionals we are alarmed by the extent of the cuts made from New York to California. Our alarm over such administrative actions should be turned into action. Library media specialists can no longer rely on claims that increasing the resources allocated to library media programs will increase program effectiveness. Continuing to justify the acquisition of more resources by keeping track of the circulation of current resources, with little regard to measuring their impact on students' success as learners, will undoubtedly continue to yield the same results. With quantitative assessments as the only data source, school library media specialists are hard-pressed to defend their programs and positions against cuts in resource allocations.

Seemingly, library media specialists leave it to school administrators to make the leap from quantitative input measures of resources and services to output measures of program effectiveness and educational outcomes. This is either an impossible task or a challenge that administrators are unwilling to accept. Adopting new guidelines for library media programs while continuing to evaluate those programs by the old method of reporting peripheral data has not produced the expected results—namely, support for library media programs by school administrators and a change in the perception of the importance of the role of library media specialists. In order to effectively implement the adopted guidelines, library media specialists need to embrace a new system of program evaluation. This technique will highlight the effectiveness of what they do in the context of learner outcomes.

THE FEATURES AND BENEFITS

Measures of effectiveness directly relate to the quality of library media programs. Measures of effectiveness correspond to the degree to which library media programs affect the achievement of the stated goals of the school district and school building. These measures reveal whether information skills are being mastered by students within the framework of an integrated approach and can provide insight into the degree to which library media programs impact content curriculum goals and content learning. The measures-of-effectiveness technique is grounded in the concept that library media specialists need to know whether the library media program is meeting its instructional goals.

Library media specialists have traditionally measured success by such indicators as circulation statistics, attendance, acquisitions, and lost or stolen books. These figures (indicators of quantity) tell only a part of the story. In order to get the attention and support of administrators, library media specialists must also measure whether student and faculty contact with library resources helped to advance the district and school goals. This additional information can be obtained through a six-part approach:

1. Determine district and school goals and objectives.

2. Determine what indicators will reflect success in achieving these goals.

3. Establish criteria of effectiveness that are meaningful to both library media specialists and administrators.

4. Adopt a scope and sequence of essential information skills that are responsive to the overall goals and objectives of the district and school.

5. Translate the scope and sequence of library and information skills into instructional action.

6. Measure effectiveness as teacher, instructional consultant, and information specialist.

These six steps transform program outputs (i.e., number of books circulated, number of classes taught, number of new acquisitions, number of interlibrary loans processed) into program inputs within a larger, more comprehensive view of assessment. For example, circulation information can be broken down into kinds of resources used for a particular teacher's assignment. Instead of being satisfied with knowing that a teacher's students used x number of materials, library media specialists need to determine that there was a positive relationship between the materials used and student success. Another example, keeping track of how many classes are taught, even within the context of an integrated unit, does not reflect the value of library media specialists to instruction. Instead, library media specialists can keep data about student confidence, efficiency, and scores as well as various indicators of teacher satisfaction. This broader-based assessment focuses on library media programs' impacts on school goals, achievement, attitudes, and behaviors.

Library media specialists are moving from reliance on indicators of quantity to measures of effectiveness (e.g., the impact of specific lessons on learner outcomes such as the effect of information skills instruction on Advanced Placement American History test results). They recognize that performance-based assessment is dependent on a series of information problems or decisions in which students are required to engage. The opportunity exists for library media specialists to reexamine their contributions to the educational process in light of recent trends in education based on learner outcomes.

Student performance has generally been assessed using a variety of student products. Assessment of learner outcomes is based on the notion that student products are responses to information-based problems or decisions. Such assessment is dependent on recognizing that students must effectively and efficiently define tasks, access information—listen, view, read—and make decisions that solve problems.

The notion that library media specialists provide expertise only through providing resources and teaching location and access skills to students and teachers severely limits the impact of information professionals within the school setting. Library media specialists can and do teach students how to determine the information requirements of assignments, provide training in on-line information access, instruct in the forms of information presentation, and assist students in determining their own effectiveness. Library media specialists can and do work with teachers to assess instructional units and lessons from an information problem-solving perspective. The wide range of possibilities for such collaboration includes ensuring the clarity of the task, providing insight into unwarranted assumptions about how students access information, and determining the appropriateness of student self-assessment strategies. From an information problem-solving perspective, library media specialists make significant and consequential contributions to successful student performance and the resultant end products.

Library media specialists should be held accountable for tangible educational outcomes. Thus, it is imperative that library media specialists clearly define the effects of quality library media programs. By these definitions, library media specialists can generate goals valued by the rest of the educational community. Additionally, specific goals and objectives within the scope of a library media program that are responsive to students' library and information skill needs can be measured against student performance. Through such measurements, library media specialists can demonstrate a direct and undeniable link to learner outcomes and consequently to the achievement of school district and building goals. Library media specialists will then be able to take credit for their direct contribution to the success of students who are required to meet performance objectives.

What library media specialists measure to describe the library media program's value is critical and reveals not only what is being measured but how effectiveness is being defined. If library media professionals are committed to the notion that they make a positive impact on learning and the achievement of school goals, then there needs to be a commitment to gathering the kind of data that give insight into validating that perception.

Inquiries that add to administrators' and library media specialists' under- standing of the real impact on overall learning include: Which courses, units, or lessons most benefit through integration with library media programs? Which instructional situations yield the best results from collaboration with library media specialists? Which programs are in need of revision and in what ways? Measures of effectiveness of library media programs can provide library media specialists with the means to determine the quality of their programs.

Program assessment based on measures of effectiveness should be ongoing and address student outcomes, district and school goals, and national guidelines. Measures-of-effectiveness assessments can help to describe what is done, how it's done, and the degree to which library media programs as implemented are responsive to user needs. The goals of program assessments can be to

- gauge the impact of library and information skills instruction;

- inform education decision makers of the theories, approaches, and specific practices that are most effective for improving student performance;

- validate the quality of existing programs or the need for change;

- forecast the need for changes in practice;
- monitor innovative approaches to improve performance;
- stimulate and focus effort on quality library media programs; and
- influence policies and decisionmaking regarding resource allocation.

THE STRATEGY

In order to accomplish these ends, the library media specialist will need to formulate an implementation strategy. The ideal plan of action will focus on the variables that affect the previously stated goals. These kinds of evaluative activities include the following:

- Define library media program objectives carefully in relation to the goals of the school and district.
- Determine what needs to be evaluated.
- Define the important variables.
- Choose a few simple but meaningful measures to assess outcomes.
- Develop the data-gathering process.
- Gather data that measure impact on learner outcomes.
- Document efforts concisely.
- Determine the degree of goal attainment.
- Examine and share the assessment results with others.

Library media specialists who engage in effectiveness assessment within the context of defined educational objectives and learner outcomes will provide a strong argument for the value of library media programs. This is the kind of information that the decisionmakers (whether administrators or taxpayers) want when they ask for accountability.

The more nearly a library media program approaches its goals within the context of school goals, the more effectively it can describe its value to student success. Measures of effectiveness can provide the kind of data that give insight into the quality of students' learning. The choice is between data as numbers derived from records and data as descriptors derived through such methods as surveys, question-naires, structured interviews, and changes in test scores. It is recognized that this approach has some disadvantages such as potential for bias, lack of information, and reluctant information providers; these kinds of factors may impact the reliability of the result. Nonetheless, measures of effectiveness can provide multiple indicators of program success.

By sharing measures-of-effectiveness information with administrators, library media specialists can encourage them to base decisions concerning library media programs upon simple yet credible data as they relate to schoolwide goals. Studies can be designed to show the effects of the library media specialist's performance and influence on the achievement of district and school goals, on student achievement, changes in teacher performance, changes in the collaborative process between library media specialists and teachers, as well as on the features of library and information skills instructional programs in relation to the achievement of specific goals and objectives and learner outcomes. These features, which are part and parcel of *Information Power*'s prescription, speak to the letter and spirit of a library media specialist's function in the school. Library media specialists must ask themselves, "Will administrators really care about library media programs unless their impact is measured?" Whatever the individual library media specialist's answer, the next logical step in implementing *Information Power*'s national guidelines is to provide information that speaks to the effectiveness of library information programs.

THE IMPACT

Performance indicators are basic to the ensurance of quality library media programs, which is a fundamental principle of *Information Power*'s mission statement. Library media specialists undoubtedly can design accountability systems that address both their own and administrators' concerns about quality instructional programs. Effectiveness assessments are fundamental to monitoring program standards and responsiveness to student needs. They are designed to elicit information about the impact of library media programs on student performance at key grade levels and can provide important information for inclusion in a total school assessment.

School library media professionals have a great deal of pride in having a clear mission with goals and guidelines to direct their professional activities; in their ability to use information resources to benefit students, teachers, and administrators; in understanding the importance of the relationships among library media specialist, teacher, student, and curriculum; and in their commitment to providing library media centers that invite both recreational and instructional use. However, pride is unpersuasive in the fight for limited resources. The real question is, What is convincing evidence that students are competent to enter the information age? What is undeniable evidence that students are achieving at higher levels because there is a library media specialist in the school? What is conclusive evidence that students are achieving at higher levels because of the quality of library media programs in schools? Boards of education, administrators, and the tax-paying public ask a more direct question: What do library media programs really do for students?

Measures of effectiveness can affect decisions about program development, collaborative planning, installation of information technologies, and facilities expansion and, in general, rally support. Library media professionals are in the best position to educate others about their value as information specialists, teachers, and instructional consultants. As school districts are forced to provide all services with decreasing budgets, library media specialists can no longer afford to believe that communities will support what they do just because they say that they make a difference. Library media specialists (practitioners and professors alike) can ensure that library media programs are positive forces within schools by gathering results-oriented data, that is, anecdotal and statistical data based on measures of program effectiveness. In this way, library media specialists will inspire confidence and trust by proving, in terms acceptable to the decisionmakers, that the scope of a library media curriculum makes a difference to the overall success of students.

CONCLUSION

In order to fulfill the mission stated in *Information Power*, library media specialists must be responsive to the concerns of school authorities. Library media specialists must prove that their worth to student learning is at least as great as that of any other member of the school professional staff. This can best be accomplished by assessing the impact of programs—not how many books are circulated and returned, how many students sit in library media center chairs, how many booktalks are given—but how well students tackle a problem and whether they know how to ask a question.

There is a growing consensus among library media specialists regarding library and information theory, instructional strategy, and curricular scope and sequence. Library media specialists are already held accountable for their programs. What library media specialists want to be held accountable for is within their control. Linking performance-based objectives and measures of effectiveness will help make library media specialists accountable in ways that will further their professional objectives while increasing the support base for programs.

The traditional indicators of quantity have not been convincing as justification for expanding, much less maintaining, existing library media center programs. *Information Power* has suggested changes in assessing library media specialists' roles and effectiveness. Accountability and the need to monitor the extent to which library media programs achieve their intended outcomes is one of those important changes. When library media specialists measure the effectiveness of library media programs on learner outcomes, they will be able to substantiate, through sound, defensible statements, that there is a strong relationship between library media programs and student success. The library media specialist who chooses to incorporate the measures-of-effectiveness concept into his or her raison d'être is the information professional who will survive in this difficult economy.

NOTES

1.   American Association of School Librarians and Association for Educational Communications and Technology, *Information Power: Guidelines for School Library Media Programs* (Chicago: American Library Association, 1988).

2.   New York State Education Department, Bureau of School Library Media Programs, "Student-Learner Outcomes" (draft) (Albany, NY: 1991).

3.   Maryland State Department of Education, School Library Media Services and State Media Services Branch, *Learning Outcomes in Library Media Services* (Baltimore, MD: 1992).

4.   Carol Collier Kuhlthau, "An Emerging Theory of Library Instruction," *School Library Media Quarterly* 16, no. 1 (Fall 1987): 23-28; "A Process Approach to Library Skills Instruction," *School Library Media Quarterly* 13, no. 2 (Winter 1985): 35-40; *Teaching the Library Research Process* (West Nyack, NY: Center for Applied Research in Education, 1985).

5.   Barbara K. Stripling and Judy M. Pitts, *Brainstorms and Blueprints: Teaching Library Research as a Thinking Process* (Englewood, CO: Libraries Unlimited, 1988).

6. Ann Irving, *Study and Information Skills Instruction* (Portsmouth, NH: Heinemann, 1985).

7. Michael B. Eisenberg and Robert E. Berkowitz, *Curriculum Initiative: An Agenda and Strategy for Library Media Programs* (Norwood, NJ: Ablex, 1988); *Information Problem Solving: The Big Six Skills Approach to Library & Information Skills Instruction* (Norwood, NJ: Ablex, 1990).

8. AASL/AECT 1988, 48.

4

Expanding the Evaluation Role in the Critical-Thinking Curriculum

 DANIEL CALLISON

The role of the school library media specialist will continue to evolve during this decade. Definitions of potential change have been suggested in recent literature[1] and reinforced through principles outlined in the current national guidelines[2] for school library programs. A model will be outlined in this essay that rests on acceptance of much that has been proposed in terms of the teaching role,[3] but this model will give new depth to the collaborative and evaluative responsibilities of the school library media specialist.

This model may not be realistic when placed against the operation of most current school library media programs. If, however, the school library media specialist is to play a leading role in development of what is truly a critical-thinking curriculum, then the evaluative aspects of this model are essential. If evaluation is limited to materials selection and does not include evaluation of student information use, the school library media specialist cannot claim to be an educator on par with the classroom teacher.

Who will teach and test in the process of evaluating (determining the value of) information? Who will teach and test selection, use, and presentation of information? The individuals or groups who hold this powerful role can define the educational demands placed on both teachers and students. The greater the access to resource services in all forms (bibliographic and human), the greater the need for critical evaluation skills. The higher the evaluation level, the greater the need for education of teachers in methods aimed toward open discussion and analysis of information use. The educational mission is not only to develop an information-wise electorate but also to increase the tolerance and patience required for frank debate of issues.

If we assume that the charge of schools (K-college) for the new age of education is to produce individuals who think, who know when they are thinking, and who think interactively with others, then curriculum design and support resources should include opportunities to practice such skills. Above all, students *and* teachers must be engaged in *critical* evaluation of the print and nonprint messages they encounter in both academic *and* nonacademic settings.

LITERACY REDEFINED

"Literacy is not simply knowing how to read and write a particular script but applying this knowledge for specific purposes in specific contexts of use."[4] "An information literate person [is one who is] able to recognize when information is needed and [has] the ability to effectively locate, evaluate, and employ the needed information."[5] "Ultimately, information-literate people are those who have learned how to learn. They know how to learn because they know how knowledge is organized, how to find information, and how to use information in such a way that others can learn from them."[6]

Literacy is a social phenomenon; its definition and its distribution shift constantly. The answers to who, what, when, and where are descriptive and simply are not answers to the questions inherent in a new definition of literacy.[7] Why? becomes the demanding question, and the literate person does not stop with one answer or with one conclusion but seeks multiple options and determines where there is overlap and conflict. The literate person knows that information in any captured form is dated, inconclusive in and of itself, and usually presented in a biased manner. Ethical considerations must be part of the solution; the presentation of support data and these considerations are at the heart of judgment methods that must be taught to those responsible for increasing literacy in our society.

The principles associated with these higher demands on a literate information-age generation must be taught at all grade levels. Methods and materials will vary, but the basic purpose should not change.

> The definition of who shall be literate also shifts. Questioning, reflecting, discussing, and writing have always been a part of literacy for talented or privileged elites. But they have rarely been a part of what we considered important for students who were not gifted or clearly college-bound. A classroom where young women, learning-disabled students, poor and minority students, all read (not recite) and write about (not copy) Shakespeare or Steinbeck is an invention that is only as old as higher education for women, *Brown* v. *Board of Education*, and rulings on the rights of handicapped students. Our expectation of high levels of literacy for many is a radical, hopeful, and demanding departure.[8]

Resnick and Klopfer[9] write that "the Thinking Curriculum is not a course to be added to a crowded program when time permits. It is not a program that begins after 'basics' have been mastered." Skills in reasoning, problem-solving, making judgments, and stating inferences need to spread from the top of Bloom's cognitive domain to all levels associated with learning. Each fact, each event, each concept, presented should have a context and be questioned to the extent that relationships to the learner's personal abilities and individual needs are acknowledged.

This is not to say that learning is without steps, levels, or that there are no prerequisites. It is necessary, however, that students become aware of such increments themselves and that they construct their intellectual webbing based on as many informational items, thoughts, or conclusions as can be made relevant to their intellectual schema and relevant to their own current and possible future social contexts.

Resnick and Klopfer suggest that construction of any student's thinking curriculum should employ the following practices in what they term *cognitive apprenticeship*.

- *Practice a real task.* Writing an essay for an interested audience, not just the teacher who will give a grade; reading a text that takes some work (asking questions, discussion, comparisons) to understand; exploring a physical phenomenon that is inadequately explained by a current concept.

- *Contextualize the practice.* Students would not do exercises on separating facts from opinions, but they would take on tasks of analyzing arguments (and statistics) on particular topics or participating in debates, both of which might engage them in a contextualized version of figuring out reliable information in a communication.

- *Observe models.* Students need plenty of opportunity to observe others doing the kind of work they are expected to learn or to do. This observation (reinforced with the challenge to evaluate or critique) gives them standards of effective performance against which they can judge their own efforts.

The thinking curriculum is based on students practicing the process of raising questions, testing a variety of possible answers, and eventually voicing, writing, constructing, sculpting, drawing, and arguing the meaning of those answers. This inquiry process is founded on gathering information for the purpose of seeking various perspectives, not just a single conclusion. Most directly, it means that students must be engaged in a conversation and be shown how to enter, contribute to, and continue that conversation on their own and with others. The literature is rich with discussion as to how such conversations can be initiated.[10] The task remaining is to show how the school library media specialist can add value to the construction of critical conversations.

ESTABLISHED IMPLICATIONS

Craver[11] has given school library media specialists a superb summary of the implications from library and information science research related to new concepts in teaching critical thinking. Critical thinking was identified in four basic areas: reading, writing, group interaction, and speaking. These are four normal activities during which students may be engaged in the gathering and presentation of information, and eventually, they may engage in a conversation about the value of the information.

Successful methods of placing students in the critical-thinking mode include the expectation that students generate their own analyses of a given text or identify, organize, and raise questions concerning issues presented. Thoughtful discussion leaders and students reacting to peer opinions in groups tend to increase critical thinking. In a discussion situation, deliberate use of waiting time conveys to students that they are expected to respond intelligently to questions. Open debate that results in capturing issues in written form should be followed by a cooling-off period in which students search for supportive evidence or counterevidence that may serve to raise the level of critical exchange.

Bowie[12] listed very tangible activities the school library media specialist and the classroom teacher can employ in order to challenge students in the reasoning process. (Her list has been paraphrased in the interest of saving space.)

- Ask a class to gather and sort opposing viewpoints on a social issue; use all possible sources; analyze merits of each opinion including the authority.

- Compile a file of popular advertisements (record television and radio spots as well) and lead students in a discussion of how information is manipulated (spoken and visual).

- Students should construct infinite bibliographies (or pathfinders) to show location of information through a variety of formats both in and *beyond* the library, including human resources.

- Create activities that require comparison of maps, charts, and census data over time and in relation to major events.

Bowie terms her activities *intervention strategies*. This term is important to note because intervention is a concept that must be broadened in the evaluation role of the school library media specialist and the teacher. The argument follows the rationale that *information use instruction* must be integrated with the curriculum in order to become effective and in order for teachers to understand its potential and relevance.

Intervention represents an opening created by the teacher or librarian in order to cue a point of instructional need. Intervention works best when collaboratively planned and classroom-content grounded. Such intervention activities should serve as models to lead to actual changes in the curriculum. The goal is to establish such critical-thinking activities at the forefront of lesson planning to the extent that the adjective *intervention* can be dropped, and inquiry activities become the curriculum. Using varied resources, raising questions, and presenting results of the information search become the standard, not the exception. Intervention by teachers and school library media specialists in inquiry activities becomes natural. Intervention becomes *the* strategy at a variety of evaluation points. Reflection on choices is found throughout the inquiry exercise, not just at the culmination of the project.

Above all, the teaching methods that work best to provide an environment for critical thinking should be used by the school library media specialist in teaching information use skills. Instead of always lecturing and saturating students with how-to facts, actively involve them in learning, let them raise problems and suggest solutions. Use cooperative or collaborative learning whenever possible so that peers can teach, learn from, and motivate each other. Supplement the library resources with access to human expertise found in other teachers, parents, or community contacts. Building activities within the limited confines of the school library is as undesirable as allowing a textbook to determine the parameters for learning. Bowie recommends her techniques for teaching critical thinking as being the responsibility of the school library media specialist and the classroom teacher. Understanding how information can be used and presented in teaching students to think[13] leads to new initiatives in curriculum development.[14]

RESTRUCTURING MEDIA PROGRAMS

In order to teach, to lead, to model, and to initiate critical thinking (not just to support, supplement, or enhance), several changes must take place in how we manage school library media programs. Many of these changes have been suggested before,[15] but the emphasis here is within the context of the information skills activities described previously, and with the understanding that the role of the school media specialist as curriculum developer will not become reality without such changes.[16] The role as evaluator of information, judge of student performance, and appraiser of the information/media/communication program becomes essential.[17]

COLLECTION DEVELOPMENT AND INFORMATION ACCESS

In order to make inquiry units that are based on critical examination of information effective, students must have access to an extensive amount of material. This means that a variety of resources should be available in terms of format, date, reading level, and points of view. There is nothing new in the idea that school library media center collections provide a variety of materials. What must be different in order to create an environment for critical examination of information is the depth of the school's library collection and the extent to which students truly have access to as many information sources as possible within and beyond the school.

First, collection development will need to take a sharp turn toward support of a few selected units. For these units, acquisition of materials should be as exhaustive as possible. Every relevant item should be acquired or access to such streamlined. More time will need to be given to discussing information needs and less time to specific (labor intensive) classification and organization of materials. Information need, information understanding, leads taken and leads rejected become the determining factors of the collection necessary for inquiry support.

Loertscher[18] has outlined such topic or unit targeting through the use of collection mapping and has argued that special instructional units simply will not take place unless there are enough resources to support one or several classrooms of students. This is a shift from the approach that *all* areas of the curriculum along with leisure reading demands should be served. Resource support for units in which critical information analysis is expected will need to be even more extensive than Loertscher proposes for library-centered events. Dramatic changes in collection priorities will need to take place.

Units shaped around critical-thinking activities will need support of files with special newspaper and magazine clippings, access to the local public and academic library collections, and acquisition of materials that may not be reviewed or evaluated by the traditional selection tools. Emphasis may need to be placed on acquiring special index resources that in turn lead to a greater use of interlibrary loan. The telephone and the fax machine may become two very important reference tools. On-line access to full-text information databases may need to be available in some classrooms as well as in the library. Checking news services may need to take place each day or each hour in some events.

Use of fiction, historical or scientific, might be necessary for some units in order to provide a social context for the more factual items gathered. Historical fiction can give the student a greater appreciation for the social events being examined, and science fiction can arouse the imagination in relation to what is actually known or theorized by scientists.[19] Oral tradition projects can result in a bonding with the community.[20]

In some cases, collections of unique resources may need to be gathered, boxed in special storage, added to over several years, and then controlled through a reserve system so that these difficult-to-obtain materials will be available to students when it comes time for the specific unit. As much as 20 percent of the annual budget might be invested over a three-to-four-year period in order to create a rich, in-depth, multiperspective collection for one critical unit. We would no longer evaluate the collection by total volumes or by the proportion of the curriculum it supports in some manner with x number of books and magazines. Evaluations would include the extent to which choice areas of the curriculum are enriched, changed, and brought to the level of critical analysis. Are the depth of the collection and the extent of reference services great enough to meet the demands of 40 or more students as each focuses on some aspect of a critical issue? Is it truly varied enough that all perspectives can be explored?

Second, the collection compiled in support of the critical information units should not be sanitized and should come, as much as possible, in its real-world packaging. For secondary school-level students, this means that tabloids and other "supermarket checkout-line materials" take a place beside the respected news magazines and newspapers usually recommended to students. It means that extremes on both sides of an issue are *easily* available. The spectrum of arguments is wide with right to left opinions. Access to factual data from government, private, and even personal records is pursued. Such massive gathering of materials would need to be relative to the information world encountered by the specific age group.

Students should have access to television programs and commentaries (previously taped and left unedited) and should view popular situational commentary found in television drama and comedy alongside the intellectual or investigative presentations. Examination of the messages delivered through popular series should be made in the context of real-world events. What are the facts, emotions, and issues raised by the situations concerning sexual harassment in television's "Designing Women" compared to charges presented during the "Thomas Supreme Court Nomination Hearings"? What are local policies and opinions concerning the issues related to sexual harassment? Can students be educated and trained to ask such difficult questions of local audiences, and can a forum be established to present their findings?

As much as possible, students should have access to government databases, statistical abstracts running back several decades, and yellow pages or specialized directories in order to contact possible experts either locally or via long distance. Yes, they need full access to the telephone or electronic mail and should be taught how to approach human resources in order to gain the information desired or needed. Interviews should be preceded with student knowledge of the basic issues, practiced interview sessions, and a specific purpose established for the interview.

Third, the long march to move materials to a centralized location called the school library media center will need to make an about face. The school library media center becomes a clearinghouse, a dissemination center, and an often-used experimental learning laboratory.[21] Classrooms will need to house and teachers will need to share informational materials as never before. In some cases, special collections of materials and artifacts for a given unit will need to be boxed and moved from one building to another as teachers select the area for the next class inquiry. Centralized district offices may serve to house such collections as well as provide centralized access to local electronic news services. Resources will flow in bulk in order to stimulate and establish the activity. Special services for seeking updated data will take students and teachers to a new insight each time the unit is processed.

Just as the new initiatives for literature-based language education depend on immediate access to and saturation with classroom sets of books, so too will units built on critical use of information demand access to resources in *both* the classroom and the library. When the unit is in full swing there should be little difference between the classroom and library resource environments other than that greater contact with resources beyond the school will be provided through the community networks maintained by the school library media specialist.

RESTRUCTURING
THE INSTRUCTION ROLE

The instructional task becomes more complex in the process of teaching critical examination of information. School library media specialists would continue to recommend the "best" or most efficient sources and search processes. In addition to this is the task of working with students to raise questions about the documentation they handle: Why did they select what they did and why did they exclude other information? What makes the information they have gleaned valuable to them and what do they need to do in order to communicate that information to others? How do they lead their audience to value what they present?

Do students need to be educated in audience analysis? Should they be aware of the limitations and expectations of the audience destined to receive their report? The answer is yes if we include "the ability to present information in such a manner as to influence others with what you know" as a part of the definition of information literacy. The instructional role moves from location skills within a safe, sanitized, preselected environment to exposure to a massive amount of varied materials and opinions. It requires practice in selection of the most useful information to answer self-generated questions,[22] and to present the findings convincingly to others.

Judgment calls, or information evaluation checks, will need to be negotiated at dozens of points, and the mediation role (teaching the meaning, the limitations, the potential of each source of information) will become extremely important—so important that both the school librarian and the classroom teacher must be experts in teaching and modeling the use of information and the decisionmaking processes.[23] Students who display the ability to make such decisions will need to be recruited into roles as peer tutors or group leaders who in turn help other students practice analysis of information.

Liesener, in response to the lack of attention to the library media field given in the government report *A Nation at Risk*, wrote, "The primary function performed by the school library media specialist or program can be viewed as a mediation function. From this perspective, the specialist plays the role of an intermediary between the incredibly complex and rapidly expanding information world and the client."[24] The mediation task in relation to teaching critical information analysis skills is so demanding that the role must be taken by the teacher as well. In units designed to immerse the student in an information flood and to teach comparison and critical selection of information, the school library media specialist and the classroom teacher must be interchangeable parts.

The teacher, as well as the librarian, teaches the quality aspects of various information sources, how to conduct an efficient information search, when to seek information beyond the library, how to compare and contrast information gathered, and how to present information effectively. The school library media specialist serves as one who *also* establishes the parameters of the assignments, defines the critical-thinking skills to be demonstrated and measured, and evaluates the student through both process and product.

Division of responsibilities would take place based on convenience for management of the activity, but the expertise relevant to selecting information, accessing information, using information, establishing assignments, and appraising student performance would be of equal merit in either camp. Such must be the shift from current roles divided between teacher and librarian if critical use of information is to move into the curriculum and become a dominant factor in molding curricular change.

The overriding goal for the curricular changes at as many ability levels and in as many disciplines as possible would be an increase in communication skills based on knowledgeable selection and use of information. Teachers and school library media specialists must have a command of (not just respect for) each other's roles in order for such dramatic changes to take place.

CHANGES IN STAFFING

In larger schools, as the shift to the full teaching role of the school library media specialist evolves and selected teachers move toward information roles, the staffing expectations for operations of the school library facility may need to change. Coordination, policy setting, and planning aspects may actually begin to rest with a "Department of Educational Resources." The chair, similar to a chair of the reading department or the science department, will act as the director of the instructional components for this new department. The chair may come from either the teaching ranks or the library media ranks, but the concentration of the chair's expertise should be in curriculum development and information management. Members of the educational resource department could be a mixture of those coming from either the library media, educational technology, or various academic backgrounds.

The concentration of the cooperative efforts would be in modeling and demonstrating instructional methods best suited for the promotion of critical-thinking skills. These include collaborative learning, free inquiry and discovery, and celebrations of student-teacher achievements within the community. The goal would be to create an environment in which teachers, students, and parents interact as a community of learners within a social curriculum.[25] Inquiry units that investigate local issues will generate the most visible community participation.[26]

Staffing for support of the resource center may include individuals who have training in the acquisition, processing, and organization of materials and who would serve the program on a paraprofessional level. The staffing cadre would include positions for clerical assistance and the usual student and parent volunteers. At least two district-level positions would become essential; one for networking of access to and acquisition of resources and the other for coordination of critical-thinking curricular efforts across all disciplines.

As the school media program has evolved over the past decades, new roles have been raised and "forced" on the school librarian without additional staffing support. Instructional television, multimedia production, instructional design, and development of integrated information skills programs have all faltered because of the lack of adequate professional staff. Development of the critical-thinking curriculum is no different. Success will depend on a full staffing commitment.

NEW INTERVENTION AND EVALUATION STRATEGIES

Although there are several useful approaches that have been recently published concerning the introduction of information search and use skills,[27] Kuhlthau's[28] observation of the "typical" library research process involving secondary school students provides the skeleton for new intervention strategies that must be practiced by both school library media specialist and classroom teacher in the critical-thinking curriculum.

Kuhlthau is refining her 1985 outline for the library research process,[29] but her basic structure is key to the approach for development of critical-thinking assignments requiring a large resource support base. Most important to her strategy is the amount of time given to laying the groundwork. Emphasis is placed on brainstorming and preliminary discussion among students, with the teacher, and with the school library media specialist. Students explore the literature, raise questions, and discuss the potential for topics before moving into the more extensive information search. Testing the information base and determining the entry-level knowledge of students are critical. The "new" approach is that students learn to self-test for such limitations or richness.

Several activities could be added or refined in this front-end portion of the Kuhlthau outline, for example, the need for priming the students through a common base of literature relevant to the general subject to be explored by the class. Textbook generalities and teacher-led discussion are not enough. Selection of important items (books, newspaper articles, films, guest lectures) should be shared by all involved in the unit in order to generate a context for the student project. From small-group discussions (led by teacher, library media specialist, and peer tutors), a common base can be identified as to what we think we know and what we have before us to explore.

MODELING CRITICAL THINKING

Too often students are placed in the position of generating products without preliminary knowledge about the issues, an understanding of the ideas or questions of their peers, or a challenge to move beyond the surface information provided in the popular media. Establishing an inquiry context includes awareness of the foundation of common knowledge and concerns, of student interest and ability levels, and of information parameters and an understanding of where an individual's own inquiry may fit or not fit with others toward the end of the process. All of these front-end considerations help novices visualize where they may eventually land at the end of the trip.

Students need access to models and examples. Not so much to tell them "this is the way it must be," but to help them visualize possibilities, critically examine products that have preceded their assignment, and challenge them to find ways to achieve better results. Modeling should come in at least two forms: peer and mentor.

Peer products from similar assignments (not necessarily identical) should be examined. Presentations might even be made by students who completed a similar project the prior semester in order to discuss fertile contacts for information, dead ends and disappointments, and the need to (and how to) plan ahead. Students should challenge information presented and be placed in a position to consider how the process and products can be improved.

> Too often teachers do what they did today because that is what they did yesterday or because that is what they think others expect them to do. Just as potters cannot teach others to craft in clay without setting their own hand to work at the wheel, so teachers cannot fully teach others the excitement, the difficulty, the patience, and the satisfaction that accompany learning without themselves engaging in the messy, frustrating, and rewarding "clay" of learning. Inquiry for teachers can take place both in and out of the view of students, but to teacher and student alike there must be continuous evidence that it is occurring. For when teachers observe, examine, question, and reflect on their ideas and develop new practices that lead toward their ideals, students are alive. When teachers stop growing, so do their students. Unfortunately, schools are seen as places where children learn and adults teach.[30]

In most current curricula, mentors modeling information use skills is almost unthinkable. In the critical-thinking curriculum, it is essential.[31] Teachers *and* school library media specialists will immerse themselves in the inquiry process as well. Each will take a slice of the area to be explored and practice the same searching, interviewing, information-gathering, and presentation tasks as those demanded of the students. Enlightenment will be the result. Insight will generate new approaches and new inquiry units. Mentors' experiences in locating and using information will be the sparks leading to multiple discussion or intervention points throughout the process. As data and counterdata, opinion and counteropinion, are gathered, questions can be raised as to levels of relevance and authoritativeness. In the end, presentations and displays will be enhanced as mentors and students share their achievements. The conversation concerning human knowledge is initiated by all learners—students and teachers.[32]

Kuhlthau describes several intervention roles of the teacher and library media specialist during the information-gathering process. These roles are so important that, again, all should be played by either of the facilitators. These key interventions are at the decision points related to information gathering. Intervention is necessary in order to assist students in selecting information, using charts and tables, understanding the context of a quotation, or tracing the roots of a given expert's true qualifications. Data may need to be verified through other print sources or by contacting a primary source whenever feasible. Just as there is guidance in focusing the inquiry, so there must be practice and guidance in selecting the information.

Guidance is necessary at the initial point of selection and at the points of deciding use, editing, revising, and presenting. A given information item may change in value at each point.

Electronic databases provide screen displays that allow teacher and student (or students) to view the results of a given search together and to question at each citation or annotation (if necessary) the potential value of the source.[33] Discussing the potential value of each source leads to discussion as to the focus of the inquiry. It continues the process of raising additional questions to explore relative to the initial research questions identified from the front-end priming literature. It reinforces the practice of critical evaluation of information.

Electronic windowing environments will increase the potential for teachers and students to exchange opinions on sources. In some future databases we may see a set of cues given that help the student select relevant sources. The credibility of a source used is one portion of the student's selection process that should be judged. Establishing credibility of a source may require intervention by teachers or librarians in their roles as information specialists. Building a case for credible, authoritative, relevant, clear, understandable evidence is a primary skill in the critical-thinking curriculum.

ADDITIONAL ASPECTS OF
ASSESSMENT AND APPRAISAL

The final stage of the Kuhlthau outline currently centers on assessing the process. Self-assessment, process assessment, and product assessment are all needed in order to determine what worked and what can be improved.

The student, as Kuhlthau describes, should reflect on the experience and verbalize what would be done differently or similarly in the next experience. Sharing projects or end results is most important in the critical-thinking curriculum. Students and teachers (including the school library media specialist) are placed in the position of presenting information to others, teaching what they have discovered, and sharing the materials in as many ways as possible beyond the library and beyond the classroom. Parents, students in other schools, local community groups, are all potential audiences. Formats can include traditional video programs, pamphlets and posters, bulletin board displays, local newspaper articles, debates, editorials, term papers, and more.

Keys to making the products valued by others include any attempt that allows the product to be seen or heard by others and celebrated in some manner (an evening open house at the school at the end of the semester to display the products of the semester's inquiry units). Maintaining a collection of many of the projects for future students to examine and use as legitimate information sources and learning devices gives the products and the producers value.

The critical evaluation process of student performance is within the role of both teacher and school library media specialist. Such evaluation requires intervention in the process at specific checkpoints with the intent to determine the progress of the student. It may be that there is a certain standard expected or the progress is measured relative to the unique entry level of each student, but the point to be established here is that judgments need to be made as to the quality of questions raised, sources pursued, evidence gathered. Biases need to be reconsidered, as well as ethical standards stemming from temptations to cloud or shade evidence through editing and lifting out of context. Use of electronic composition will open a new world for mentor intervention. Comments can be fed into electronic outlines and screen displays as they are constructed. Electronic mail will allow students to see critical comments at home as well as at school, and they can respond immediately.

Evaluation should be made concerning the ability of students to *add value* to their education experience. They are able to move from an entry point to some other level because of this experience. Knowledge gained through the experience should transfer to other areas of their learning environment. What do students know at the end that they did not know at the beginning? What questions remain beyond the culmination of this project that they would like to explore? Evidence that the student took the initiative to continue the process, either on a new set of questions or in another discipline or another assignment should be documented. We cannot measure lifelong learning, but we can measure changes within a student's academic life.

Process assessment should include examination of the merits of resources identified and used and considerations for seeking access to resources that seemed initially beyond reach. Did the student make the extra effort to obtain what was previously off limits? The critical-thinking curriculum should allow for exposure to similar information channels encountered in real life as well as those hidden or even unknown at the beginning of the process. What tools best enable students and teachers to sort through information in order to construct their knowledge and eventually convey a message to others? Are these tools easily available for the next set of students?

Project assessment should lead to development of other units as well as to refinement of the one just completed. Questions should be raised concerning overlap or duplication of assignments, transfer of skills or building on skill levels, and how demanding the project was in terms of placing students in the position to make critical information judgments. This evaluation process should engage the opinions of several teachers and administrators. It should include those who are considering development of such units for the first time. The evaluation process thus becomes a learning and a teaching activity in itself. This process results in the bricks that construct the new units of the critical-thinking curriculum.

The purpose of the interventions is to create an opportunity to engage the student concerning information choices and use. The goal is to nurture novice information specialists in their communications (librarian-to-teacher, teacher-to-student, student-to-student, and other cycles that allow learning within a social exchange).[34] A new cast of information access and use experts should evolve from the student population, and their role as educators of other students should be recognized and rewarded.

Evaluation at each point can include a testing instrument. Tangible performances[35] can be identified and should be measured[36] along with a narrative record of teacher, librarian, and student observations. Two points are necessary to remember, however. First, teachers as information specialists (including classroom teachers and the school library media specialist) should administer the evaluation and determine the merits of the experience. Second, evaluation should include the process and may even emphasize the process *over* the product.

New methods of evaluation should be explored because students may be judged on questioning techniques, search and location strategies, listening skills, organization skills, scripting and editing skills, and presentation methods. Just as a house is appraised and valued at several stages of construction, so too is the process by which students and teachers construct knowledge and intelligence from the information surrounding them. Foundation, framework, and finished product each have need for new appraisal instruments and new collaborative appraisers who have an inquiry method orientation.

NOTES

1. P. Turner, *The School Library Media Specialist's Role: Helping Teachers Teach* (Littleton, CO: Libraries Unlimited, 1986); K. W. Craver, *The Changing Instructional Role of the High School Librarian* (Champaign, IL: University of Illinois, Graduate School of Library and Information Sciences, 1986).

2. American Association of School Librarians and Association for Educational Communications and Technology, *Information Power* (Chicago: American Library Association, 1988).

3. K. Haycock, *The School Library Program in the Curriculum* (Englewood, CO: Libraries Unlimited, 1990).

4. S. Scribner and M. Cole, *The Psychology of Literacy* (Cambridge: Harvard University Press, 1981), 15.

5. M. M. Huston, "Introduction: Toward Information Literacy—Innovative Perspectives for the 1990s," *Library Trends* 39, no. 3 (Winter 1991): 187.

6. P. S. Breivik, chair, *Final Report of the American Library Association Presidential Committee on Information Literacy* (Washington, DC: H. W. Wilson, 1989), 1.

7. L. Resnick, *Education and Learning to Think* (Washington, DC: National Academy Press, 1987).

8. D. P. Wolf, *Reading Reconsidered: Literature and Literacy in High School* (New York: College Entrance Examination Board, 1988), 3.

9. L. B. Resnick and L. E. Klopfer, eds., *Toward the Thinking Curriculum: Current Cognitive Research* (Washington, DC: Association for Supervision and Curriculum Development, 1989).

10. G. Hillocks, ed., *Research on Written Composition: New Directions for Teaching* (Washington, DC: National Institute of Education, 1986); M. A. Laughlin, H. M. Hartroonian, and N. M. Sanders, eds., *From Information to Decision Making: New Challenges for Effective Citizenship* (Washington, DC: National Council for Social Studies, 1989); T. Holt, *Thinking Historically: Narrative, Imagination, and Understanding* (New York: College Entrance Examination Board, 1990); D. P. Wolf and N. Pistone, *Taking Full Measure: Rethinking Assessment Through the Arts* (New York: College Entrance Examination Board, 1991); D. P. Wolf, *Reading Reconsidered: Literature and Literacy in High School* (New York: College Entrance Examination Board, 1988); E. A. Silver, J. Kilpatrick, and B. Schlesinger, *Thinking Through Mathematics: Fostering Inquiry and Communication in Mathematics Classrooms* (New York: College Entrance Examination Board, 1990); D. Prentice and J. Payne, *More Than Talking* (Caldwell, ID: Clark, 1983).

11. K. W. Craver, "Critical Thinking: Implications for Library Research," in B. Woolls, ed., *The Research of School Library Media Centers* (Castle Rock, CO: Hi Willow Research and Publishing, 1990), 121-34.

12. M. Bowie, "The Library Media Program and the Social Studies, Mathematics, and Science Curricula: Intervention Strategies for the Library Media Specialist," in B. Woolls, ed., *The Research of School Library Media Centers* (Castle Rock, CO: Hi Willow, 1990): 21-48.

13. J. C. Mancall, S. L. Aaron, and S. Walker, "Educating Students to Think," *School Library Media Quarterly* 15, no. 1 (Fall 1986): 18-27.

14. M. E. Eisenberg and R. E. Berkowitz, *Curriculum Initiative* (Norwood, NJ: Ablex, 1989); C. J. Krimmelbein, *The Choice to Change: Establishing an Integrated School Library Media Program*, ed. P. K. Montgomery (Englewood, CO: Libraries Unlimited, 1989); Wisconsin Educational Media Association, *Online Information Retrieval: Teaching Electronic Access in the Curriculum* (Manitowac, WI: WEMA, 1989).

15. J. Stroud, "Library Media Center Taxonomy: Further Implications," *Wilson Library Bulletin* 56, no. 6 (February 1982): 428-33; K. E. Vandergrift, *The Teaching Role of the School Library Media Specialist* (Chicago: American Library Association, 1979); K. W. Craver, "The Changing Instructional Role of the High School Library Media Specialist: 1950-84," *School Library Media Quarterly* 14, no. 4 (Summer 1986): 183-92.

16. D. V. Loertscher, *Taxonomies of the School Library Media Program* (Englewood, CO: Libraries Unlimited, 1988).

17. D. Callison, "Evaluator and Educator: The School Media Specialist," *Tech Trends* 32, no. 5 (October 1987): 24-29.

18. D. V. Loertscher, "Collection Mapping: An Evaluation Strategy for Collection Development," *Drexel Library Quarterly* 21, no. 2 (Spring 1985): 9-21.

19. M. Lentz, *Nuclear Age Literature for Youth* (Chicago: American Library Association, 1990).

20. E. Wigginton, *Sometimes a Shining Moment: The Foxfire Experience* (Garden City, NY: Anchor, 1986).

21. D. Callison, "School Library Media Programs and Free Inquiry Learning," *School Library Journal* 32, no. 6 (February 1986): 20-24.

22. E. R. Kulleseid, "Extending the Research Base: Schema Theory, Cognitive Styles, and Types of Intelligence," *School Library Media Quarterly* 15, no. 1 (Fall 1986): 41-48; D. Carr, "Living on One's Own Horizon: Cultural Institutions, School Libraries, and Lifelong Learning," *School Library Media Quarterly* 19, no. 1 (Fall 1991): 217-22.

23. C. Markuson, "Making It Happen: Taking Charge of the Information Curriculum," *School Library Media Quarterly* 15, no. 1 (Fall 1986): 37-40.

24. J. W. Liesener, "Learning at Risk: School Library Media Programs in an Information World," *School Library Media Quarterly* 13 (Fall 1985): 14.

25. K. G. Short and C. Burke. *Creating Curriculum* (Portsmouth, NH: Heinemann, 1991).

26. K. Sheingold, "Keeping Children's Knowledge Alive Through Inquiry," *School Library Media Quarterly* 15, no. 2 (Winter 1987): 80-85.

27. C. Haycock, "Information Skills in the Curriculum," *Emergency Librarian* (September-October): 11-18; H. L. Jay, *Stimulating Student Search* (Hamden, CT: Library Professional Publications, 1983); M. E. Jay and H. L. Jay, *Designing Instruction for Diverse Abilities* (Hamden, CT: Library Professional Publications, 1990); B. K. Stripling and J. M. Pitts, *Brainstorms and Blueprints* (Englewood, CO: Libraries Unlimited, 1988); M. B. Eisenberg and R. E. Berkowitz, *Information Problem Solving* (Norwood, NJ: Ablex, 1990).

28. C. C. Kuhlthau, *Teaching the Library Research Process* (West Nyack, NY: Center for Applied Research in Education, 1985).

29. C. C. Kuhlthau, "An Emerging Theory of Library Instruction," *School Library Media Quarterly* 16, no. 1 (Fall 1987): 23-28.

30. R. S. Barth, *Improving Schools from Within* (San Francisco: Jossey-Bass, 1990), 49-50.

31. J. Bavell, *Teaching for Thoughtfulness* (New York: Longman, 1991).

32. *The Information Power Video* (Chicago: Encyclopaedia Britannica Educational Corporation, 1988), 19 minutes, color video program. Comments from John Goodlad in the introduction; K. D. Andrasick, *Opening Texts* (Portsmouth, NH: Heinemann, 1990). See chapter 2, "Enabling Critical Conversation."

33. D. Callison and A. Daniels, "Introducing End-User Software for Enhancing Student Online Searching," in A. Lathrop, comp., *Online and CD-ROM Databases in School Libraries* (Englewood, CO: Libraries Unlimited, 1988), 128-46.

34. J. C. Harste, K. G. Short, and C. Burke, *Creating Classrooms for Authors* (Portsmouth, NH: Heinemann, 1988); R. Routman, *Invitations: Changing as Teachers and Learners K-12* (Toronto: Irwin, 1991).

35. F. M. Newman, "Higher Order Thinking in Teaching Social Studies: A Rationale for the Assessment of Classroom Thoughtfulness," *Journal of Curriculum Studies* 22, no. 1 (1990): 41-56.

36. S. P. Norris and R. H. Ennish, *Evaluating Critical Thinking* (Pacific Grove, CA: Midwest Publications, 1989).

5

Assessing the Library Research Process

 Carol Collier Kuhlthau

The final task of students in the library research process is to evaluate what they have done. They need to review their progress throughout the process to identify what caused them difficulty and to determine what they might do differently to improve their process as well as the presentation of their findings.

The purpose of evaluation is to identify what learning has taken place and where further instruction and practice are needed. The traditional assessment of a research assignment is the teacher's evaluation of the research paper or other form of presenting the findings of library research. A grade on a research paper is a limited indication of the specific learning that has taken place in the research activities or of the further instructional needs of students. Evaluation of the end product of library research rarely identifies specific weaknesses and strengths in the library research process of students.

Self-assessment of the research activities can enable students to pinpoint particular problems and can lead to improvement and new learning. Self-evaluation, of course, does not take the place of the teacher's evaluation. Students' assessment of their own research activities and the teacher's evaluation of the product of library research go hand-in-hand to help students improve their research process.

Evaluation should take place immediately following the completion of the research assignment. The entire process should be fresh in students' minds when they reflect on their progress. Prompt feedback is an essential component of learning. Self-assessment and the teacher's evaluation should be planned as the last stage of the library research process.

Students need to be introduced to strategies and techniques that reveal the research process for examination. This program offers a number of ways to assist students in assessing their library research process.

Reprinted from *Teaching the Library Research Process*, 2d ed. (pp. 172-178) by Carol Collier Kuhlthau. Metuchen, NJ: Scarecrow Press. Copyright 1994. Used with permission.

FEELINGS OF STUDENTS AFTER
THE RESEARCH PROCESS

When students look back over their library research, they often experience either a feeling of accomplishment or a sense of disappointment. If they have been able to locate and present information on their focus in a way that meets the requirements of the assignment, they usually feel satisfied. Some students will be pleasantly surprised at the results they have been able to produce. Many will want to talk about their research projects, enthusiastically explaining their focus and the findings of their library research.

Students experience a sense of disappointment when their expectations of the results of their library research have not been met. These students frequently have not identified a focus during the research process and have not been successful in supporting or presenting a focus in their research paper.

INCREASING SELF-AWARENESS

Self-awareness can lead students to view themselves more objectively. When they become more objective in assessing their progress in library research, they are better prepared to learn from their mistakes and successes. They need to be objective in assessing their own research activities. This program has been planned to make students more aware of their process while they are moving through the stages of a library assignment.

Assisting students to reflect on their experience in working on a research assignment helps to reveal their research process to them. Students are often surprised when they discover the various stages they have come through. One student described discovering stages in the research process in this way: "Well, I guess there are three phases. . . . I never realized that I did this. I never realized I did all the work in three phases. I just thought I did all of the work the last minute and did my report."

Once students are aware of having experienced stages in the library research process, they are able to plan their library research activities accordingly. Their approach to library research becomes more realistic, efficient, and effective. They begin to build their thoughts on their topics within the various stages of the library research process.

There are four elements in the research process that students need to become more aware of in their assessment at the end of a research assignment. The elements are the evidence of a focus, use of time, use of sources, and use of the library media specialist. An awareness of their use of these elements in library research can enable students to improve their approach to future research assignments.

EVIDENCE OF A FOCUS

After a research assignment has been completed, students should assess the presentations of their library research findings for the evidence of a focus. The focus of the research paper should be clearly stated in the introduction and supported in the body of the paper with the facts and ideas collected from library sources.

Many students' research papers lack a clear focus. As one student described it, "I had a general idea but not a specific focus. . . . As I was writing I didn't know what my focus was. When I finished, I didn't know what my focus was. . . . I don't think I ever acquired a focus. It was an impossible paper to write." Students need to become aware of the difference that a focus makes in a research paper. They can learn to identify a focus early in the research process.

Students should be able to express their focus clearly and succinctly at the end of a research assignment. A fairly accurate test of the presence of a focus is being able to state the focus after the assignment has been completed. Students with unfocused papers tend to name the general topic when asked to tell what their paper was about. When asked to describe the focus of his paper, one student stated, "I don't know. I did have one. It had to do with transcendentalism and the essay on self-reliance more than anything else. . . . I guess it was transcendentalism and Emerson." Another student had similar difficulty stating the focus of her paper. "It was just Fitzgerald and his books." Students who have a clearly identified and supported focus tend to state the focus of their paper rather than the general topic. One student clearly described the focus of her paper, "I decided to show how the place itself (Brook Farm) helped the people to use the ideas of transcendentalism to make the community work."

By assessing the presence of a focus in their papers, students learn the function of a focus. They become more aware of the mistakes they made in presenting the focus as well as the success they had in supporting the focus. In this way, they learn the importance of forming a focus early in the research process, which they can develop and support through the information they collect from library sources.

USE OF TIME

An important element in the assessment of the research process of students is how they paced themselves in their library research. Students need to become aware of the way they use their time in a research assignment. The best time for students to consider the research process as a whole and assess their use of time is shortly after the assignment has been completed.

Many students think that they procrastinated until shortly before the assignment was due and then they did all of their research in a short span of time. However, when they reflect on what has actually taken place in the early stages of the research process, they are often surprised to find that rather than procrastinating, they were thinking and learning about their topic in a general way.

As students assess their pace in a research assignment, they become aware of the stages they have progressed through to develop their research presentation. The student who explained that he had not realized that he did all of the work in three phases, but thought that he put it off until the last minute, was becoming aware of different stages in the library research process. By assessing their research activities, students can become aware that at the beginning their thoughts about their topic are developing. Next, they are exploring for a focus and finally they are collecting information pertaining to their focus. As students assess their use of time in a research assignment, they can learn to pace themselves effectively in future library research.

USE OF SOURCES

The way the sources in the library collection have been used is an important consideration in assessing students' library research. At the completion of a research assignment, students should recall the order in which they used sources. Were the sources used randomly or were sources used in a logical sequence?

Students can become aware of the sequence in which they used library sources. Using general sources first and working toward the more specific sources matches the stages of the research process. At the beginning of the process, general sources help students to learn about the topic. As they explore for a focus, sources on various aspects of the topic need to be used. After a focus has been formed, information must be collected from sources with specific information about the focus. Students can learn to develop patterns of use that proceed from general to specific sources.

One student described discovering the use of sources in this way: "The ones [sources] in the middle are most useful because in the beginning you're not definitely sure what you are doing. Then as you get direction toward the middle, you know what you are looking for. In the end you are just looking for extra things so you are sure you have everything, but a lot of it is repeat."

Students can become familiar with different ways to use sources in the various stages of the research process. For example, the library catalog can be used in each stage of the process at a different level and for a different purpose. It is important for students to become aware of the intricacies of using library sources and indexes and to become more proficient at using sources for a variety of purposes. They need to reflect on their research activities to assess their use of library sources through the different stages of the process.

USE OF THE LIBRARY MEDIA SPECIALIST

In assessing their research activities, students need to reflect on their use of the library media specialist. Students' expectations of how a librarian might help them are often either too high or too low. Some students expect a librarian to produce the sources that are the key to their library research assignment immediately. Others avoid asking for help and attempt to be totally independent in their library research. They need to become aware that neither extreme fosters the best use of the library media specialist.

Students can review the stages of their research process and analyze their use of the librarian at each stage. As they recall the problems that they encountered, they should consider how the librarian might have helped them. They can become aware of the different levels of information need at the various stages in the research process and can assess their requests for information at each stage. They can learn how to ask for information and to practice stating requests that enable the librarian to be helpful to them. Here is how one student described her inability to use library sources as a result of a reluctance to seek the assistance of a librarian: "I went to the university library and I really didn't get anything out of that because it was so huge that I didn't know where anything was."

Students can learn to use the librarian as one of the resources in the library. They must learn not to be overly demanding by asking for information that they can readily locate themselves. On the other hand, they need to think of the librarian as an access point to the collection and an expert on library research. Interaction with the librarian is part of the library research process and students can learn when and how to request information from the librarian.

TECHNIQUES FOR ASSESSING THE RESEARCH PROCESS

The library research process is an individual endeavor that is difficult for students or teachers to assess without some way of exposing it for observation. A number of techniques for helping students observe their research process are offered in this book. Each of these techniques reveals the research process to enable students to become more aware of their own progress through the stages, to identify problems, and to take steps toward improvement. The activities offered in this chapter, construction of a time line and a flow chart, and conferences and writing, are ways of reviewing the research activities for assessment.

TIME LINE

Throughout this program, the time line of the research process has been used to help students visualize the stages in the process and to identify where they are in the process as they proceed through the stages. When students have completed the research assignment, they can personalize the time line by drawing one for their own research process.

By drawing a line across a piece of paper and identifying the initiation of the assignment at the far left and the completion of the presentation at the far right, students have a blank time line on which to reveal their research process. They can refer to their journals to recall events and dates to be placed on their time lines. Their time lines should show when they chose their topic, when they explored for their focus, when they formed their focus, when they collected information, when they completed their library research, and when they prepared their presentation.

This technique reveals to students the stages in their own library research process. In this way, they can assess their use of time during the stages of their research. When stages of the library research process become apparent to students, they are able to plan better use of their time in future research assignments.

FLOW CHART

The flow chart, like the time line, reveals the entire research process to students. The flow chart, however, is not confined to the stages of the research process but includes additional details of the students' library research.

Students are given a piece of paper with one box in the upper left corner and another box in the lower right corner. The first box is labeled "received assignment" and the other box is labeled "wrote paper." Students make a flow chart of connecting boxes to show how they progressed through the library research process. Each connecting box reveals a step they took to complete their library research assignment. Students can use their journals to help them recall the progress of their research.

On the flow chart, students can show when they used the library, what sources they located, how their thoughts about their topic evolved into a focus, and the steps they took in collecting information. The chart depicts a detailed analysis of the library research process from beginning to end.

Constructing a flow chart gives students an overview of their research activities. They can readily visualize the library research process as a whole when it is charted on one sheet of paper. This overview offers students a way to assess their progress and to identify problem spots. They can begin to analyze the steps they took and determine what they might do differently the next time they are assigned library research or when they research something on their own.

CONFERENCES

Conferences with the teacher or the librarian at the completion of the research assignment are extremely effective for helping students to recall and assess their own research activities. By using such techniques as the time line and the flow chart, students can describe their library research. In this way, stages and steps in the library research process that are commonly overlooked or ignored can be examined and evaluated. The teacher or librarian can offer specific recommendations for improving the library research.

Students benefit from the one-to-one guidance offered in a conference. Conferences do take considerable time, but for new researchers the rewards can be substantial. When students talk about their library research process with the teacher or the librarian using the recommended devices to reveal the various steps and stages, learning often takes place that is both lasting and transferable.

WRITING A SUMMARY STATEMENT

Students' ability to write about their focus after the research assignment is completed is a good way to assess the presence of a focus in their research. If they have identified and presented a clear focus, they are likely to be able to write about the focus in a brief summary statement. On the other hand, if their presentation was unfocused, they are likely to have difficulty stating a focus.

By writing a summary paragraph to explain the findings of their library research, students become more aware of their focus or lack of focus. They begin to understand how a focus affects their thinking about a topic. Being able to express succinctly what their research was about is evidence that a focus was present. Students who are aware of the function of a focus are apt to seek one in future library research. A clear focus enables them to make a summary statement about their topic.

ROLE OF THE TEACHER

An essential element in teaching is evaluating learning. The teacher, as an experienced evaluator, plays a significant role in helping students assess their own library research process. Students need guidance in viewing their library research to determine their successes and weaknesses.

By using techniques recommended in this book, teachers can help students assess their own library research activities. Holding individual conferences to discuss a student's time line or to help a student construct a flow chart are excellent ways to reveal the library research process for evaluation and for identifying particular problems and strengths. Students need guidance in examining how they used their time in the library research activities. They need assistance in examining how they developed and supported their focus. Teachers can guide secondary students to visualize their own library research process and to identify problem areas needing attention.

ROLE OF THE LIBRARY MEDIA SPECIALIST

Library media specialists should be involved in the assessment of the research process. As experts on library research activities, as well as the sources in the library collection, they can help students identify problems and recommend strategies for improvement.

Students need help to view the library as a whole and to assess their use of sources in relation to the variety of sources available. Library media specialists can introduce sources that might have been used but were not. Students also need help in identifying times in their library research when the librarian might have been helpful and been turned to as a resource.

The roles of the teacher and the library media specialist overlap somewhat in helping students to assess their library research process. They work as team to guide self-evaluation. It is important that they share responsibility in offering students conferences and other strategies for students' assessment of their own library research process.

6

Alternative Assessment
Promises and Pitfalls

 DELIA NEUMAN

Assessing what students have learned and how well they have learned it is an ongoing challenge for instructors and policymakers alike. There is widespread and often heated discussion and debate concerning two divergent approaches. Proponents of national standardized testing argue the importance of their cause; advocates of testing reform contend that standardized testing is both inadequate for assessment and damaging to curricular and instructional practice. Each side of the debate attracts ardent supporters, but those who champion so-called alternative assessments seem to be gaining an increasingly sympathetic audience.

This chapter provides an overview of the alternative assessment movement and its relationship to the school library media specialist (SLMS). It begins with a discussion of the criticisms of standardized testing that generated the movement and continues with presentations on the theoretical assumptions of alternative assessment, on the emerging body of research and practice related to specific alternative assessment models, and on criticisms of alternative assessment. The chapter concludes with a discussion on the implications of the approach for SLMSs and suggestions regarding a context they might adopt to foster the productive use of alternative assessment.

CRITICISMS OF STANDARDIZED TESTING

By the 1930s, standardized tests had become an accepted feature of most U.S. schools, although their scope and status in public education were relatively small (Grady 1992; Perrone 1991). The use of standardized testing has spiraled since the 1950s and 1960s, however; by the end of the 1980s the approach had become so prevalent "that U.S. public schools administered 105 million standardized tests to 39.8 million students during the 1986-87 school year. . . . At that rate, by the time a student graduates, he or she has [taken] 30 standardized tests" (Neill and Medina 1989, 688).

As the numbers and kinds of standardized tests have mushroomed, murmurs about the inadequacies of this approach to student evaluation have become a roar. Psychometricians, who have wrestled with the technical dimensions of test design for decades, continue to struggle with a variety of serious issues. (See, as just one

Reprinted from *School Library Media Annual, 1993* (pp. 13-21) by Carol Collier Kuhlthau, ed. Englewood, CO: Libraries Unlimited. Copyright 1993. Used with permission.

example, the December 1989 issue of *Educational Researcher*, which is devoted to educational assessment.) Critics of the testing establishment over the years have repeatedly noted racial, ethnic, gender, and socioeconomic biases in various versions of various tests and decried the placement (and exclusion) of students according to test results (Haney and Madaus 1989; Neill and Medina 1989; Perrone 1991). Recently, the political uses of test results have been roundly condemned by a number of writers (for example, Darling-Hammond and Wise 1985; Kirst's interview with Shepard, 1991; Koretz 1988; Neill and Medina 1989; Shepard 1989; and Smith 1991) who have observed school districts' attempts to appear like Garrison Keillor's Lake Wobegon—"where *all* the children are above average." Shepard (1989) summarized the ultimate effects of the use of test results for political purposes, for which, of course, the instruments were never designed:

> In the United States today, standardized testing is running amok. Newspapers rank schools and districts by their test scores. Real estate agents use test scores to identify the "best" schools as selling points for expensive housing. Superintendents can be fired for low scores, and teachers can receive merit pay for high scores. Superintendents exhort principals and principals admonish teachers to raise test scores—rather than to increase learning. Occasionally school boards issue a mandate that "all students must be above the national norm," which, absurdly, is the same as requiring that 100 percent of students be above the 50th percentile. (4)

Criticisms of the political uses of standardized test scores have received more popular attention, but criticisms of the negative effects of standardized testing on student learning also fill the professional literature. Authorities note that such tests typically employ a multiple-choice format—a pattern implying that knowledge consists simply of identifying the one and only correct answer to a question formulated by someone else. This reductionist approach distorts learning in several ways. First, it focuses on discrete elements rather than emphasizing the context and complexity of true understanding. Furthermore, it suggests that the omniscient test designer is the final authority on these unitary answers and—more important—on what questions should be asked. By implication at least, standardized tests thus negate the value of teachers' and students' generating and solving their own intellectual problems in context. The underlying approach is seriously at odds with current learning theories, which highlight the importance of the active construction of one's own knowledge (Raizen and Kaser 1989; Shepard 1989; Wiggins 1989).

Finally, because teachers, schools, and whole systems are judged by how well their students perform on standardized tests, their ultimate effect is to drive curricular and instructional decisions that foster learning at the lowest levels: In order to fare well in comparison to other schools and students, educators must train their own students to be effective test-takers and regurgitators of facts rather than masters of problem-solving and other critical-thinking skills. "Teaching to the test," acknowledged as an unavoidable consequence of any kind of assessment, is especially pernicious when the tests measure only students' skills in rote memorization rather than their ability to analyze, synthesize, and evaluate various kinds and levels of information (Grady 1992; Haney and Madaus 1989; Kirst's interview with Shepard, 1991; Neill and Medina 1989).

Even the critics of standardized tests acknowledge their technical improvement (if not their greater appropriateness) in recent years: Commercial test designers have become more sensitive in their sociology and more sophisticated in their ability to tap higher-order skills. Nevertheless, proponents of performance assessment would argue, years of overreliance on standardized tests and on teacher-made instruments that mimic their formats have created serious negative effects both within and beyond the classroom.

THE PHILOSOPHY OF
ALTERNATIVE ASSESSMENT

The alternatives to standardized testing proposed by various individuals and groups go by many names: Performance assessment, authentic assessment, direct assessment, and portfolio assessment are among the most frequently mentioned. Whatever form or title such approaches assume, they share several common and overlapping elements. First, they are grounded in a philosophy that the direct assessment of student achievement is superior to the indirect assessment provided by tests. Tests measure only "surrogates," or indicators of what students know; direct assessments examine actual student products—essays and other writing samples, problems generated and solved by students, exhibits prepared by students, and similar artifacts. Such assessments are said to yield an authentic and comprehensive understanding of students' patterns of achievement rather than only the secondary, single, and static measure provided by a stanine score (Grady 1992; Wiggins 1989; Wolf, Bixby, Glenn, and Gardner 1991).

Second, alternative assessments are designed to be ongoing, natural parts of students' experiences instead of singular and stressful additions faced at the end of a given year or semester. Rather than being divorced from meaningful day-to-day learning (as commercially produced "high-stakes" standardized tests are seen to be), alternative assessments are tied directly to classroom work. They become opportunities to correct errors or remedy flaws in an emerging product, allowing students to engage in the process of building toward a polished final outcome. Because students will follow a similar create-revise-perfect process in their future work environments, alternative assessment is thought to prepare them more appropriately for their after-school experiences (Grady 1992; Perrone 1991; Wiggins 1989; Wolf et al. 1991).

Third, alternative assessment reaffirms the role of the teacher rather than the test designer as the primary director of students' learning. In most models, students' assessors are also their instructors: The instructor designs, administers, and evaluates the assessment, diagnosing the students' learning needs as well as their achievements as an organic part of the evaluation process. Because the assessors are responsible for meeting those needs, they are also expected to design appropriate instructional strategies as an inherent part of the assessment process. In alternative assessment, then, the instructor reclaims the central professional role of the educator who has responsibility for the student's educational experience from its beginning to its end (Grady 1992; Perrone 1991; Wiggins 1989).

Fourth, because students are to be involved in establishing the assessment tasks and criteria, alternative assessment provides direct experience for students in using higher-order thinking skills, in participating actively in their own learning, and—ultimately—in taking responsibility for that learning. This focus on the student's direct and purposeful involvement is consistent with current cognitive theory, which holds that deep understanding occurs only when learners actively construct their own knowledge rather than passively absorbing facts and ideas presented by others (Grady 1992; Wiggins 1989; Wolf et al. 1991).

These direct and natural ties to teaching and learning are seen as the primary advantage of alternative assessment. The assessment becomes not simply a means of evaluating students' competencies at a single point in time but a powerful teaching and learning tool that has value throughout a course, semester, or school year. By intertwining teaching, learning, and evaluating, alternatives to traditional assessment are cited as means of restoring the integrity of the student's educational experience as a seamless and meaningful whole.

ALTERNATIVE ASSESSMENT IN RESEARCH AND PRACTICE

Portfolio assessment has long been a staple in college writing programs and in continuing-education programs for adults that grant academic credit for so-called life experiences. More widespread attention to alternative assessments in public education, however, is a fairly recent phenomenon: It has appeared and begun to flourish in concert with other contemporary movements toward educational reform. Efforts of organizations as diverse as the National Assessment of Educational Progress, the National Commission on Testing and Public Policy, the Educational Testing Service, the Coalition of Essential Schools, the National Council of Teachers of Mathematics, and the Association for Childhood Education International (among others) have provided the impetus and, in some cases, guidelines for the development of alternative assessment models. In the mid to late 1980s, a variety of prototypical programs began to appear, and several of these are repeatedly mentioned as exemplary.

At the state level, Maeroff (1991) cited California, Connecticut, Kentucky (which is planning to have the first statewide assessment completely based on performance by 1995), Rhode Island, and Vermont as leaders in the movement toward alternative assessment. California has been developing alternative assessment models for writing, literature, mathematics, science, and history-social science at various grade levels. Connecticut is focusing on performance-based assessments in science and mathematics for its prospective high school graduates (Shepard 1989). New York State introduced performance-based assessment of fourth-grade science students in 1989 (Goldman 1989). Rhode Island's still-small pilot program "embraces outcomes in reading, writing, speaking, listening, and mathematics" (Maeroff 1991, 274) for third-graders. Vermont's approach, which has been evaluated by the RAND Institute on Education and Training, involves fourth- and eighth-graders who compile examples of their work in portfolios for writing and mathematics (Koretz et al. 1992).

Pittsburgh's Arts Propel project—cited as "the nation's most extensive districtwide experiment in using portfolios" (Goldman 1989)—is detailed here because it provides a particularly robust example of the nature, conduct, and outcomes of performance assessment. Funded by a five-year Rockefeller Foundation grant, the project involved Harvard University's Project Zero and the Educational Testing Service as well as the Pittsburgh Public Schools and focused on three interrelated modes of alternative assessment: projects, portfolios, and reflective interviews. Projects designed to illustrate "independent problem solving in the arts" consisted not only of final versions of students' visual arts creations but also of preliminary sketches and other items documenting the emergence of students' ideas within those projects. Projects became part of portfolios—designed to illustrate "the processes that underlie long-term development"—which generally included "several projects (in order to provide a wide sampling of work) as well as independent work, a journal or sketchbook, or whatever other materials provide information about the student's (or group's) artistic development during a given report period, semester, or year" (Wolf 1987/1988, 27). Finally, reflective interviews based on the portfolios—designed in part so that "students judge themselves"—provided teachers an opportunity to assess students' progress and final levels of understanding while giving students a venue for examining the range of their work and arriving at their own conclusions about what they had learned.

Other projects, districts, and individual schools have also initiated alternative assessment efforts. For example, Project Spectrum—the Harvard-Tufts experiment in reconceptualizing intelligence on the basis of Howard Gardner's (1983) theories of multiple intelligences—uses continuing alternative assessments in Gardner's seven areas (mathematics, science, music, language, visual arts, movement, and social skills) as the basis for developing an annual student profile that describes each student's activities, strengths, and weaknesses and includes suggestions for follow-up activities (Krechevski 1991). The Saturn School of Tomorrow, an experimental school within the St. Paul (Minnesota) School District, uses no grades or marks but relies on portfolios and presentations to assess each student's progress according to an individualized Personal Growth Plan (King 1992).

Other examples also exist. Simmons (1990) reported on the use of portfolio assessments in fifth-grade language arts; Raizen and Kaser (1989) discussed the inclusion of alternative assessments in elementary science programs. Rogers (1989) offered a variety of suggestions for alternative assessments based on his work with the social sciences curriculum in a number of elementary schools. Although local programs seem scattered at present, with some 40 states planning to include alternative assessments (usually writing samples) at the state level (Maeroff 1991), activity at the local level can only increase.

CRITICISMS OF ALTERNATIVE ASSESSMENT

Even proponents of alternative assessment counsel caution at this early stage in the development of its theory and methodology (see, for example, O'Neil 1992 and Worthen 1993). Furthermore, the movement is not without its outright critics (see, for example, Cizek 1991). Published research on the approach is sparse, and evaluation results are mixed. Psychometricians have raised serious questions about establishing the validity, reliability, generalizability, and comparability of assessments conducted according to methods that are so individualized and dependent upon human judgment (Koretz et al. 1992; Linn, Baker, and Dunbar 1991; Moss 1992). Questions of fairness in designing and applying criteria have also been raised. The lack of training in assessment theories and techniques by those who would administer the assessments increases the likelihood of errors and misinterpretations. And, of course, the extraordinary amount of time (and therefore the high cost) required to implement a program of alternative assessment has not gone unnoticed (Maeroff 1991).

Wolf (1987/1988), commenting on the interim results of the Arts Propel project, echoed others who have analyzed performance assessment efforts. After citing such exciting results as teachers' and students' enthusiasm about the knowledge and insight gained from the experience, she went on to address the concerns that make even advocates of the approach acknowledge the impediments to its widespread and effective use:

> The concepts of projects, portfolios, and interviews have to become reliable procedures that can be used by a wide range of teachers with students of varying ability levels. Researchers and teachers have to investigate just which aspects of student learning to document. Equally important is the work of helping educators to come to common, reliable assessments of the materials that students generate in their projects, portfolios, and interviews. Not least of all, there is the question of how such qualitative modes of assessment can "fit" within the demands of classroom life, let alone the confines of college admissions folders. (29)

IMPLICATIONS FOR THE
LIBRARY MEDIA SPECIALIST

Despite such concerns about the nature and implementation of alternative assessments, the approach is clearly finding a place within the arsenal of schools' evaluation techniques. And although there is little evidence to date of any widespread involvement of school library media centers in the movement, it seems clear that the SLMS will be strongly affected by this emerging educational practice. On the one hand, SLMSs might well wonder whether this approach is the agent by which formal student evaluation will sneak through the library media center door; on the other, however, the fact that SLMSs believe and habitually function in ways that are consistent with the alternative assessment approach suggests that—once again—the SLMS has an untapped wealth of experience and expertise to offer other members of the instructional team.

Library media center programs are grounded in many of the same assumptions that undergird alternative assessment; indeed, SLMSs traditionally rely on alternatives to tests and grades to evaluate students' progress. They have extensive experience in directly assessing students' information-seeking efforts, in negotiating the content and criteria for those efforts, and in helping students construct polished final products. Both in theory and in practice, alternative assessment and the library media center are highly compatible.

At a fundamental level, the philosophy of alternative assessment parallels that of the information specialist in general and the SLMS in particular: Both philosophies assume that *using* information—rather than simply *possessing* it—is the most important component of intellectual activity. More traditional assessment strategies require students to *own* particular facts and concepts, at least long enough to reiterate them in a particular format; alternative assessment models require students to manipulate, evaluate, and present information in meaningful ways. This requirement clearly mirrors *Information Power*'s (AASL/AECT 1988) statement that the SLMS's mission is "to ensure that students and staff are effective *users* [emphasis added] of ideas and information" (1). *Information Power* is hardly a manifesto for the alternative assessment movement, but its grounding in similar assumptions provides theoretical support for the involvement of the SLMS.

In addition, both alternative assessment and *Information Power* focus on the *process* of learning and stress students' continuing growth toward increasingly complex understandings. Such growth implies far more than the simple mastery of isolated pieces of data and indeed assumes the development of critical-thinking skills and the active construction of meaningful knowledge. Not surprisingly, the literatures of both the school library media field and the alternative assessment movement concentrate on these important dimensions of students' experience.

The affinity between alternative assessment and the library media center extends beyond theoretical assumptions and into the realm of practice. As a process-oriented approach, alternative assessment relies on three core strategies: observing students' work, interviewing them about their changing perceptions and understandings, and analyzing the documents they prepare (Raizen and Kaser 1989; Rogers 1989). These strategies are also, quite obviously, hallmarks of the daily instructional efforts of the SLMS. Moreover, they are the key data collection strategies of qualitative inquiry, an approach gaining increasing prominence in education as a whole and in school library media work in particular (see Aaron, Kroll, and Mancall's report on Treasure Mountain III, the school library media research retreat conducted in fall 1992). Designed to elicit deep understandings of complex processes and situations, these powerful techniques are highly appropriate both to alternative assessment and to the ongoing work of every SLMS.

That work provides the SLMS with extensive experience in the basic procedures of alternative assessment. In helping students devise and refine their search strategies, the SLMS engages in a dialectic designed to determine both the content of students' learning and the criteria students will use to determine their success. In helping students find increasingly targeted information, the SLMS guides students' efforts to locate and evaluate the information they will need as they move through the stages of constructing polished final products. Clearly, the entire process of information skills instruction assumes the ongoing and direct assessment of students' efforts with the goal of constantly improving their skills.

Wolf et al. (1991)—in their extensive, informative, and provocative discussion of alternative assessments—suggested that "the design and implementation of these new forms of assessments will entail nothing less than the transition from what we call a 'testing culture' to an 'assessment culture' " (33). Such a culture would rely on new understandings of learning and intelligence, new standards of evidence, and "a new psychometrics" (63) that ensures both sensitivity and rigor in the application of alternatives to the standardized tests that currently drive and structure educational practice. What these authors did not say, however, is that such an "assessment culture" already exists: It is inherent in effective school library media center programs.

Once again, then, the SLMS community has the opportunity to enlighten the rest of the education community about the media specialist's actual and potential roles. As schools continue to discover the value of including alternative assessments in their overall student evaluation efforts and as they continue to struggle with ways to implement these assessments with wisdom and sophistication, much of the theoretical and practical guidance they seek is available in the library media center. An SLMS committed "to provid[ing] the leadership and expertise necessary to ensure that the library media program is an integral part of the instructional program of the school" (*Information Power*, 26) should see the alternative assessment movement as an opportunity to promote both students' learning and the media center's expertise.

REFERENCES

Aaron, S., C. Kroll, and J. Mancall, eds. *Researcher Practitioner Partnerships: Applying Qualitative Methodologies to School Settings.* Unpublished Proceedings of Treasure Mountain III. (Contact Hi Willow Research and Publishing, P.O. Box 266, Castle Rock, CO 80104.)

American Association of School Librarians and Association for Educational Communications and Technology. *Information Power: Guidelines for School Library Media Programs.* Chicago: American Library Association, 1988.

Cizek, G. J. "Innovation or Enervation? Performance Assessment in Perspective." *Phi Delta Kappan* 72, no. 9 (1991): 695-703.

Darling-Hammond, L., and A. E. Wise. "Beyond Standardization: State Standards and School Improvement." *Elementary School Journal* 85, no. 3 (1985): 315-36.

Gardner, H. *Frames of Mind: The Theory of Multiple Intelligences.* New York: Basic Books, 1983.

Goldman, J. P. "Student Portfolios Already Proven in Some Schools." *School Administrator* 46, no. 11 (1989): 11.

Grady, E. *The Portfolio Approach to Assessment.* Bloomington, IN: Phi Delta Kappa, 1992.

Haney, W., and G. Madaus. "Searching for Alternatives to Standardized Tests: Whys, Whats, and Whithers." *Phi Delta Kappan* 70, no. 9 (1989): 683-87.

King, D. T. "The Saturn School of Tomorrow: A Reality Today." *T.H.E. Journal* 19, no. 9 (1992): 66-68.

Kirst, M. W. "Interviews on Assessment Issues with Lorrie Shepard and James Popham." *Educational Researcher* 20, no. 2 (1991): 21-27.

Koretz, D. "Arriving in Lake Wobegon: Are Standardized Tests Exaggerating Achievement and Distorting Instruction?" *American Educator* 12, no. 2 (1988): 8-15, 46-52.

Koretz, D., D. McCaffrey, S. Klein, R. Bell, and B. Stecher. *The Reliability of Scores from the 1992 Vermont Portfolio Assessment Program: Interim Report.* Los Angeles: RAND National Center for Research on Evaluation, Standards, and Student Testing, 1992.

Krechevski, M. "Project Spectrum: An Innovative Assessment Alternative." *Educational Leadership* 48, no. 5 (1991): 43-48.

Linn, R. L., E. L. Baker, and S. B. Dunbar. "Complex, Performance-Based Assessment: Expectations and Validation Criteria." *Educational Researcher* 20, no. 8 (1991): 5-21.

Maeroff, G. I. "Assessing Alternative Assessment." *Phi Delta Kappan* 73, no. 4 (1991): 272-81.

Moss, P. A. "Shifting Conceptions of Validity in Educational Measurement: Implications for Performance Assessment." *Review of Educational Research* 62, no. 3 (1992): 229-58.

Neill, D. M., and N. J. Medina. "Standardized Testing: Harmful to Educational Health." *Phi Delta Kappan* 70, no. 9 (1989): 688-97.

Nickerson, R. S., ed. Educational Assessment (Special issue). *Educational Researcher* 18, no. 9 (1989).

O'Neil, J. "Putting Performance Assessment to the Test." *Educational Leadership* 49, no. 8 (1992): 14-19.

Perrone, V. "On Standardized Testing." *Childhood Education* 67, no. 3 (1991): 131-42.

Raizen, S. A., and J. S. Kaser. "Assessing Science Learning in Elementary School: Why, What, and How?" *Phi Delta Kappan* 70, no. 9 (1989): 718-22.

Rogers, V. "Assessing the Curriculum Experienced by Children." *Phi Delta Kappan* 70, no. 9 (1989): 714-17.

Shepard, L. A. "Why We Need Better Assessments." *Educational Leadership* 46, no. 7 (1989): 4-9.

Simmons, J. "Portfolios as Large-Scale Assessment." *Language Arts* 67, no. 3 (1990): 262-68.

Smith, M. L. "Put to the Test: The Effects of External Testing on Teachers." *Educational Researcher* 20, no. 5 (1991): 8-11.

Wiggins, G. "A True Test: Toward More Authentic and Equitable Assessment." *Phi Delta Kappan* 70, no. 9 (1989): 703-13.

Wolf, D. P. "Opening Up Assessment." *Educational Leadership* 45, no. 4 (1987/1988): 24-29.

Wolf, D., J. Bixby, J. Glenn, III, and H. Gardner. "To Use Their Minds Well: Investigating New Forms of Student Assessment." *Review of Research in Education* 17 (1991): 31-74.

Worthen, B. R. "Critical Issues That Will Determine the Future of Alternative Assessment." *Phi Delta Kappan* 74, no. 6 (1993): 444-54.

7

Assessment of Student Performance
The Fourth Step in the Instructional Design Process

 Barbara K. Stripling

This chapter explores one component of Philip Turner's instructional design model, which is pictured here. Specifically, the chapter provides information to help the reader

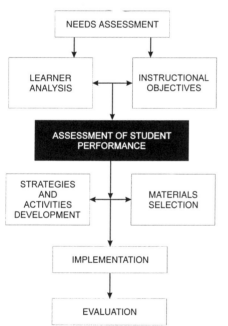

- understand the integration of assessment and instruction;

- recognize the characteristics of authentic assessment;

- understand the advantages of authentic assessment;

- create the classroom conditions for authentic assessment;

- know the types of authentic assessment;

- write authentic tests;

- plan portfolios as a means of authentic assessment;

- plan performances as a means of authentic assessment;

- understand assessment through teacher-student personal contact; and

- incorporate teacher and student reflection into the assessment plan.

Reprinted from *Helping Teachers Teach: A School Library Media Specialist's Role*, 2d ed. (pp. 140-151) by Philip M. Turner. Englewood, CO: Libraries Unlimited. Copyright 1993. Used with permission.

The instructional design process consists of eight steps described in a program developed by Turner (1993). The fourth step in the instructional design process is planning the assessment of student performance. Traditionally, this assessment has been conducted through locally produced or nationally standardized testing. Because testing often does not provide a complete picture of students' achievements (revealing only a limited view of students' knowledge at a particular point in time), educators are augmenting or replacing traditional testing with assessment that is ongoing, open-ended, and in a real-life context. This type of assessment is often referred to as authentic assessment.

Despite the shift in the methods of assessment, the characteristics of good assessment have not changed: Assessment must measure how well students have mastered the objectives; assessment must be reliable (accurately reflecting students' abilities and not a particular evaluator's idiosyncrasies); assessment must allow students to demonstrate what they know rather than what they do not know; assessment must provide feedback to teachers on the effectiveness of instructional techniques, materials, and activities.

THE PURPOSE OF THE STUDENT ASSESSMENT STEP

Assessment must be considered as a stage of the instructional design process because assessment is integral to any instructional unit. Assessment plans will influence the activities and materials as well as the instructional strategies to be used. Teachers may plan to assess student progress and teaching effectiveness either formally or informally at any point during the unit.

Four questions can guide the development of an asessment plan: (1) What do we want students to know and be able to do? (2) What will count as acceptable performance? (3) How can we ensure expert judgments? and (4) How can we provide feedback? (Diez and Moon 1992). Teachers must answer these questions during this stage of the instructional design process. If an English teacher, for example, wants students to connect themes in the literature they are studying with specific values held by the society at the time, the teacher must make a series of decisions. First, the teacher must decide how students can best demonstrate their understandings— through an essay, a talk-show script, a travel-back-in-time brochure, or some other product. Second, the teacher must select or create models to show students the standard of performance expected. Third, the teacher must design evaluation rubrics with descriptions of behavior for each level of performance in order to ensure reliable judgments from evaluators, which could include fellow students, teachers, or community members. Finally, the teacher must decide how and when to give feedback and whether to include peer comments, opportunities for revision, conferencing, and student self-evaluation.

CHARACTERISTICS OF
AUTHENTIC ASSESSMENT

Authentic assessment can encompass various techniques including testing, questionnaires, interviews, ratings, observations, performance samples, and work products (Chittenden 1991). Authentic assessment often involves a performance of some kind, but it is not authentic unless "the student completes or demonstrates the desired behavior . . . in a real-life context" (Myer 1992). Authentic assessment can be conducted at any point in a unit and for any level of instructional objectives. In other words, if a teacher wants to assess student performance on low-level objectives in the middle of a unit about the Middle Ages, the teacher might ask each student in a testing situation to select and explain the facts about life in the Middle Ages that wuld be most important to portray in a television miniseries, with rationales for those decisions. The teacher's high-level objectives for the final project of the unit might be assessed by asking students to create an actual script for an episode in the miniseries. The script should make the Middle Ages come alive.

To be a reliable picture of a student's understandings, authentic assessment must be ongoing, measuring student performance throughout out the process of learning. Some research has shown that from eight to twenty samples are required to produce a reliable assessment of an individual's problem-solving ability in a given content area (Herman 1992).

Authentic assessment is a learning experience in itself. Unlike generic multiple-choice tests that categorize and limit the options, authentic assessments must be open-ended to allow many different approaches and products. Students are expected to synthesize, to use their learning to create new ideas during the assessment process.

Peters (1991) has said that authentic assessment must be based on authentic content, and he has suggested five guidelines for selecting authentic content:

1. Material should be based on important concepts. Teachers should decide the essential themes and ideas to be learned; assessment should be directly related to these ideas.

2. Material should be consistent with state, school district, and school curriculum guidelines. This consistency will enable students to make connections with what they have previously learned and with what they are being taught in other subject areas.

3. Material should have real-life experience as its basis. Students should expect to encounter problems and concepts that have application to the world outside the school environment.

4. Material should take into account the developmental progression of students and build on prior knowledge. Teachers must determine when needed background is missing and then must include that information in the course content.

5. Material should demand a high level of thinking from the students.

An essential component to authentic assessment is reflection, by both the teacher and the students. Students must be asked to appraise their own learning and to reflect on their strengths and weaknesses. In some authentic-assessment formats (portfolios, for example), students start the process of assessment by setting goals for their own learning. They end the process in metacognition as they evaluate their own progress, their level of thinking, and their uses of processes and strategies to accomplish the goals they have set. Teachers must reflect on the appropriateness of the assessment for the content being taught and on the effectiveness of activities and instructional strategies.

CONDITIONS FOR AUTHENTIC ASSESSMENT

The learning environment in the classroom must allow the characteristics of authentic assessment to flourish by nurturing the students' complex thinking and reflection, by establishing assessment as a learning experience in itself, and by valuing students' progress as well as final achievements (Zessoules and Gardner 1991). Newmann has identified four additional classroom conditions that are essential for authentic assessment to take place: collaboration, access to tools and resources, discretion and ownership, and flexible use of time (Newmann 1991). In a collaborative classroom, students help one another accomplish the learning objectives. Students recognize that they are expected to perform to a standard of achievement; they will not be weighed one against another during evaluation. Projects often entail group work, although each individual is held accountable for mastering all the learning objectives. Teachers in a collaborative classroom regard students as partners in the learning process and invite participation by other teachers and community members.

A second condition for authentic assessment is that students must be free to use whatever tools and resources they need. Because the assessment involves creative thinking beyond rote learning, teachers must allow students to use information sources for details and specifics, just as the students would have those sources available in real-life, problem-solving situations. Students can consult a handbook of mathematical theorems, a chart of chemical properties, the textbook, class notes, library sources, even experts in the field, because the teacher is measuring the students' understanding and ability to manipulate information in creating new ideas, not the students' memorization of specific facts.

The classroom that fosters authentic assessment involves students in the learning and in the assessment process. Students help decide what is important and how their achievements should be measured. For example, a key characteristic of portfolios is that the students select the components and justify their choices in a reflective introduction to each piece. In performance assessments, once the teacher has structured an authentic situation, students have great leeway in determining the framework and content of their own performance.

Finally, the authentic classroom allows flexible use of time. Every student is expected to perform to a standard; some students may take longer to reach it than others. One student may take seven weeks to complete a project and another only three, but both are allowed the time necessary to achieve the standard. Projects are not arbitrarily ended because a grading period is over or because the teacher initially predicted completion in a shorter amount of time.

An ongoing, daily commitment to authentic assessment in the classroom changes the very nature of the curriculum. Consider, for example, a low-level math classroom in the junior high or high school in which students are struggling with calculations that they should have learned in elementary school. A typical instructional plan for teaching measurement to these students, for example, might involve large-group instruction, individual practice by working all the measurement problems in the book, and then a multiple-choice test. A plan based on authentic assessment might include instruction in measurement; individual or group practice by measuring items in the classroom and figuring out logical proportions for furniture and room size; and group performance by designing, measuring pieces for, and constructing a dollhouse for an elementary classroom. Although the assessment of learning is much more difficult when students construct a dollhouse than when they take a test, the learning is probably more interesting, involving, and effective for the students.

TYPES OF AUTHENTIC ASSESSMENT

Four main categories of authentic assessment can be identified: tests, portfolios, performances, and personal contact with the student.

Tests

Grant Wiggins (1989, 1992) has suggested that for tests to be authentic assessment, they must be designed using eight criteria:

1. The test must measure essential content, something that is meaningful for the student to learn. It should concentrate on areas that are usually ignored, such as problem solving, thinking, and writing, and should stress depth rather than breadth. The test should not be an interruption in the learning process but should stimulate the thoughtful use of knowledge.

2. The test should include enough samples that it is a valid measure of what it purports to measure. Students must be allowed to show their strengths. Only then can generalizations be drawn about a student's abilities.

3. Scoring should be based on essential elements to understanding, not on what is easiest to measure. The scores should be multifaceted, not a single grade. Self-assessment is an important component.

4. Standards should be established that are reasonable for the real world, not arbitrarily easy for the school. Tests should never be graded on the curve.

5. The problems on the test should have detailed, enticing, realistic contexts so that students enjoy thinking about and working on them. Students with different learning styles should be allowed to approach the problems in their own way.

6. The tasks on the test should be validated by giving them to a small group of students or teachers before the administration of the test. Items that are confusing or that do not seem to measure the objectives should be eliminated or revised.

7. The scoring should be reliable and possible. Scoring rubrics can be constructed to increase reliability.

8. The results of the assessment should be used by students, teachers, and administrators to facilitate future learning and improve the learning environment.

Murray (1990) has suggested some variations to the prevalent one-student-per-test-at-the-end-of-the-chapter testing. Students might get second chances or access to additional information. The teacher might give an exam in class but then allow students to have a second copy of the exam to work on at home with their open textbooks. The students will discover answers to the questions that troubled them on the earlier exam. Other teachers use take-home exams. In one variation, students receive the questions before the test. They can take the questions home and prepare, then write the exam in class without referring to their notes.

Other suggestions by Murray include various group-testing situations. In one, students work together to figure out answers to thought-provoking questions. Students compose a group answer, but in Supreme Court fashion, individuals can file dissenting opinions. In another situation, students work in groups to discuss multiple-choice test questions and teach each other. Students fill out their own answer sheets based on their group work.

Murray (1990) also suggests that students can work in pairs to take tests. Students answer some of the test questions on their own but combine into randomly selected pairs to work an equal number of questions (although each student still maintains an individual answer sheet). A suggested variation is an essay test on which students work in pairs to write one essay answer to each question (Murray, 1990).

In summary, authentic tests must follow the guidelines identified for authentic assessment. Tests must measure important content, not incidentals. Tests must require thinking; simple repetition of memorized facts is boring and useless to the students and the teacher. Tests must require students to apply their understandings to real-life situations. Until students can work with the information they have acquired, they have gained no understanding of the material. Although tests may be relatively easy to grade (compared to portfolios and performances), authentic tests can be extremely difficult to construct.

Portfolios

Portfolios are selected collections of students' work. The students have control over their portfolios—they set the initial goals for their portfolios; they select the works to be included based on criteria they have established; they often write introductions in which they assess their own learning and their understanding of the subject concepts; and they write reflective pieces about each work included (Paulson, Paulson, and Meyer 1991). A portfolio reveals a student's understandings, abilities, progress, and mental processes. Students can compile portfolios for their entire school program or for individual classes.

Portfolios are student-directed; therefore, students learn to assume responsibility for their own learning. Teachers who have tried portfolio assessment have discovered that students compile their best work with pride, holding themselves accountable for higher standards than if they were simply turning in teacher-directed assignments for a grade. Students willingly revise pieces for their final portfolio based on revision comments from teachers and peers. Students are also effective evaluators of their own progress when they write reflective essays about their portfolio work. Students have commented that they learn almost as much from their reflections as they do from the original work.

Given the previous listed guidelines, portfolios can vary a great deal in their content and form. Vavrus (1990) has suggested some questions that teachers and students will answer as they compile their portfolios.

• What will the portfolio look like?

The portfolio can be arranged in several different ways—chronologically, topically, by format, by rate of success (worst to best). It can be in a folder, a box, or any other container. The only requirement is that it should be planned to match the goals for the portfolio.

• What should go into a portfolio?

The portfolio should include work that demonstrates mastery of the goals set by the student and teacher. It can include finished work only or all drafts and revisions as well as the finished work. Students must include pieces of self-reflection. Some portfolios contain only written work, but in a variety of formats including essays, tests, learning logs, journals, creative pieces, and samples of homework. Other portfolios contain videotapes of student performances, artwork, audiotapes, videodiscs, Hypercard stacks, and whatever else the students feel demonstrates their proficiency.

• When and how do students select the work to be included in the portfolio?

The teacher and students should set up a time line at the beginning of the year for final portfolio completion. Individual pieces are added as the students select and revise them during the year. The final work on the portfolios should be finished in time for the students to present them to the teacher, an evaluation panel (if used), their peers, or their parents.

Students select the works based on their own and the teacher's goals. If the teacher's main goal is to see growth in understanding of themes of history, the students should select work on the themes of history from various points during the year. If a student's goal is to develop creativity, the portfolio should also include the student's creative pieces from throughout the year.

• How will the portfolios be evaluated?

The teacher sets standards of performance that would be acceptable outside of the school. Work in the portfolios is judged against those standards, probably through the use of a rubric that contains descriptive phrases rather than evaluative comments. For example, for a history unit on change, an excellent student essay might be described as "Demonstrates solid knowledge of the social, economic, and political disruption caused by change. Has developed a personal understanding of the effects of change on people's lives. Expresses concepts and feelings in understandable language and with conviction." A mediocre piece might be described as "Demonstrates knowledge of the surface effects of change on society (changing fads and fashions) but does not connect those effects with changes in the social, economic, and political structures. Appreciates change only as it happens to other people at other times; has made little personal connection to the concept of change. Expresses concepts and feelings understandably but with little personal conviction." The rubric might also include the following description for a poor piece: "Displays little understanding of the concept of change and the effects of change on society. Offers no personal insight into change; has formed no personal connection to the unit. Expresses ideas in a manner that cannot be easily understood by others."

With such a rubric, evaluations can be conducted reliably by the classroom teacher, other teachers, students, and community members. Many teachers have discovered that by opening up the evaluation process, they help the students see that their work is preparing them for the world outside the classroom. That understanding adds value to their classroom work.

Portfolios should be evaluated according to external standards, but that evaluation can be tempered with an assessment of student growth. More than any other method of assessment, portfolios offer teachers the opportunity to see student growth in ideas, skills, and attitudes. When students document how much they have learned, they can be rewarded through the assessment process.

- What should be done with portfolios after the year has ended?

Once portfolios become more widely accepted in our schools, teachers will have the opportunity to review students' portfolios from previous years, which will help them gain a clear picture of students' abilities. With this insight, teachers can structure a curriculum that builds on the skills that most students have already developed and emphasizes those areas where students have faltering skills. A higher degree of individualization is also possible when teachers have access to students' portfolios. Students who can write a cogent, well-organized essay at the end of one year can be directed to more sophisticated essays the next year.

Performances

Some learning is best demonstrated in performances. Certainly drama, music, speech, physical education, and athletics require performances in order for students to demonstrate they have acquired the skills and processes basic to those subject areas. Other subject areas can profit from performance-based assessment as well. Students in English can act out a play they have written about the current conflicts in South Africa. Business-law students can debate the issue of punishment for white-collar crime. Third-graders can test the properties of water in its three states: solid, liquid, and gas. Students in history can videotape a "Sixty Minutes" report on the signing of the Emancipation Proclamation.

In order for performance assessment to be authentic, it must be based on real-life experiences and authentic content. Students can perform individually or in groups. They may perform for their classmates or for a larger audience. They may be evaluated by the teacher, their peers, or outside evaluators, which could include other teachers, parents, or community members.

The advantages of performance assessment are many. Students create their own performance; they are not restricted by prewritten questions. Although some rote learning may be involved, students develop larger understandings of the issues and concepts while they are preparing their performances. Students are learning in depth; they will remember the issues presented in their performances long after they have forgotten specific facts. Performances boost students' self-esteem and enhance communication skills. Most important, students enjoy the learning that takes place during the preparation and performance.

Performance assessments have some limitations as well. They are generally culminating activities; therefore, they must be combined with other forms of assessment to give a clear picture of student progress throughout a unit or semester. Performances require more in-class time and effort on the part of both the students and teachers than do tests or portfolio pieces. It can take days for each student to have a chance to perform. Performances are messy and loud; students are not "in their places" as they write, rehearse, and perform. It is difficult to make performance assessments valid so that they measure the skills and concepts intended and so that the evaluator can generalize about a student's abilities. Research has shown that many samples are needed before such assessments can lead to generalizations.

The most serious limitation of performance assessments is the difficulty of assessing them reliably. Mehrens (1992) has identified four problems with performance-assessment reliability. First, the scores tend to be quite subjective based on who is doing the scoring and what is regarded as important. Writing is the most developed form of performance assessment; with extensive training, evaluators for written work have finally achieved some reliability. Other forms of performance assessment are not as well developed. What is known is that persons who have a vested interest in the scores should not rate the performances. Therefore, teachers should not evaluate the performances of their own students.

Second, Mehrens points out that it is difficult to compare performances to external standards. Performances are often rated on a scale; however, the scale may reveal how well a student performed compared to other students rather than how well the student achieved according to specific criterion-referenced standards.

Mehrens also argues that it is extremely difficult to equate performance assignments between classes and from one year to the next. The situations for performances must be changed each year to prevent rote repetitions of supposedly creative interpretations. But the difficulty arises when teachers try to make a situation from one class equal to a different situation in another class or year.

Finally, because many performances are group situations, teachers must wrestle with the problem of assessing the individual versus the group performance. They must decide how to assign an individual grade in addition to the group evaluation.

Despite the limitations, teachers are incorporating performances into their instructional units. Consideration of the skills needed for the performances must be given early in the instructional design process so that teachers can incorporate concepts, skills, materials, and strategies to prepare students for their eventual performance. Students who anticipate a performance tend to be focused and excited about the learning. Performances invigorate the classroom.

Personal Contact with the Student

Because the reliability of assessments is enhanced by increasing the number of samples, teachers may choose to supplement testing, portfolios, and performances with assessments garnered through personal contact with the student. These personal assessments include questionnaires, interviews, and unobtrusive observations. All make the assessment process more interactive, with the students contributing ideas, strategies, and attitudes that may not be obvious to the teacher in other assessment situations. Interactive assessment is intended to discover the conditions that will help a student grow, not simply to document a student's progress to that point (Brozo 1990).

A diagnostic interview, used already by reading teachers, can help the teacher understand students' interests and strengths. The teacher can discover if students have a clear understanding of the goals and expectations for a unit. The student can use the teacher as a sounding board to test out new ideas and strategies or to clear up confusing issues. The teacher can conduct a formal assessment interview, recording progress on various criteria and suggesting areas to pursue, or can use the interview more informally to help the student establish a focus and overcome deficiencies.

Questionnaires can be informal and simple. For example, a teacher might hand each student an index card during the last five minutes of class time. Students write comments in response to a question such as "What is the most important idea that you learned today?" or "How will you use what you learned today to create your final product?" Teachers can also use more formal questionnaires to help students assess their own progress to that point. Although questionnaires provide assessment information about each student, they may actually be more valuable in providing data on the effectiveness of the unit in progress. With such valuable feedback, teachers can make adjustments in content or pace to accommodate students who are having problems.

Observations may be the most powerful form of personal assessment. Students can keep a learning or research log in which they include their successes and frustrations. Teachers can keep a journal with observations about specific students and the class as a whole. Teachers can target a specific behavior and record observations related to that behavior for each student (for example, care with laboratory equipment). Teachers can simply record group dynamics during a class period and review their notes later for insights into how well the groups are functioning. The strength of using student and teacher observations is that they are usually honest representations of the situation; they have not been manipulated by the assessment instrument itself.

Personal contact with the student provides valuable information to the teacher and important feedback to the student throughout the instructional unit. It is a formative assessment strategy that should accompany the summative strategies of tests, portfolios, and performances.

AUTHENTIC ASSESSMENT AS
REFLECTION IN ACTION

A shift from traditional assessment to authentic assessment causes changes in teacher and student behavior as well as in the learning environment. Students take a more active role in their own learning. They plan it, carry it out, and evaluate their own progress and success. They reflect on their own performance throughout the learning experience and change their behavior based on their reflections. Students work collaboratively with other students. Finally, students understand the connections between what they are learning and the real world.

Teachers are also more reflective. They use feedback to change what is happening in the classroom. They foster collaboration among students and with other teachers and community members. Teachers use high standards in assessing student work, basing their benchmarks on expected performance outside of school. They expect students to gain the abilities they need to succeed once they have graduated.

The learning environment of an authentically assessed classroom is more open to resources and technology beyond the classroom and the school (school and public libraries are essential here). Instructional time is flexible enough to allow students to pursue subjects in depth. Students are expected to demonstrate their proficiency through performances or portfolios in addition to testing.

Authentic assessment, with its emphasis on real-life learning and reflection, changes the teaching strategies and content of instructional units. Selecting the type of assessment to be used helps educators continue the instructional design process through the stages of materials selection, activities development, implementation, and evaluation.

LEVELS OF INVOLVEMENT BY THE
LIBRARY MEDIA SPECIALIST AT THE
ASSESSMENT OF
STUDENT PERFORMANCE STEP

The Initial Level

Although the library media specialist is not directly involved in the instructional plan at this level of involvement, the idea of authentic assessment is new enough to most teachers that the library media specialist can have a profound impact by building a professional collection of materials for the teachers to consult and by booktalking these during faculty meetings. The library media specialist can also serve as a clearinghouse for articles on assessment. Particularly interesting articles can be collected and distributed to interested faculty. The library media specialist may organize a discussion group in which each member reads and reports on articles. By typing and distributing notes from those meetings, the library media specialist can provide each interested faculty member with a written summary of relevant articles on assessment.

One offshoot of authentic assessment that has received particular attention is portfolios. The library media specialist can subscribe to a portfolio newsletter, collect portfolio articles, and perhaps contact a school using portfolios to borrow samples to serve as models for interested teachers.

Because authentic assessment involves learning in depth, students often need to use library materials. The library media specialist at the initial level provides access to these materials and develops the collection based on student needs. Participation in interlibrary loan or a fax network for sharing periodical articles allows the library to meet increased demands caused by authentic assessment.

The following is a list of works on assessment that are recommended for the professional library:

Anthony, R., T. D. Johnson, N. I. Mikelson, and A. Preece. (1991). *Evaluating Literacy: A Perspective for Change.* Portsmouth, NH: Heinemann.

The authors provide a philosophy and a practical action plan for changing assessment from mere testing to an ongoing, authentic process that involves students, teachers, and parents in a variety of different assessment techniques. Although the book focuses on literacy assessment at the elementary grades, all the ideas could easily be adapted to other subject areas and grade levels. Ordering information: $17.50 from Heinemann Educational Books, 361 Hanover St., Portsmouth, NH 03801-3959.

Archbald, D. A., and F. M. Newmann. (1988). *Beyond Standardized Testing: Assessing Authentic Academic Achievement in the Secondary School.* Reston, VA: National Association of Secondary School Principals.

This monograph discusses the assessment of authentic academic achievement through measuring proficiency in language, analysis, problem solving, and specific curriculum content; through exhibitions; and through portfolios and profiles. Ordering information: $8.00 (pbk.) from National Association of Secondary School Principals, 1904 Association Dr., Reston, VA 22091.

Assessment Alternatives Newsletter.

The focus of this newsletter is to offer assessment alternatives so that educators can select the appropriate technique for each learning situation. Each issue contains short articles, descriptions of assessment projects, and an annotated bibliography of assessment resources. Ordering information: Subscriptions are $25.00/year. Order from Northwest Evaluation Association, 5 Centerpointe Dr., Suite 100, Lake Oswego, OR 97035.

Association for Supervision and Curriculum Development. (1991). *Educational Leadership,* 48(5).

This issue focuses on higher educational standards and includes several articles on assessment. Ordering information: Subscriptions are $32.00/year. Single copies are $5.00. Order from Association for Supervision and Curriculum Development, 1250 N. Pitt St., Alexandria, VA 22314-1403.

―――. (1992a). *Educational Leadership,* 49(8).

The whole issue features articles about using performance assessment and portfolios. Ordering information: Subscriptions are $32.00/year. Single copies are $5.00. Order from Association for Supervision and Curriculum Development (see previous address).

―――. (1992b). *Redesigning Assessment.* Alexandria, VA: Association for Supervision and Curriculum Development.

This twenty-minute video shows classrooms that rely on performance-based assessment using portfolios, presentations, and exhibitions. The tape portrays the effectiveness of these alternative assessment techniques in creating a climate of thoughtfulness and excitement for learning. The video is accompanied by the sixty-page *Facilitator's Guide.* Ordering information:

$228.00 purchase for ASCD members, $278.00 for nonmembers. $120.00 rental for five days. Preview tape is available for $20.00. Order from Association for Supervision and Curriculum Development (see previous address).

Belanoff, P., and M. Dickson (eds.). (1991). *Portfolios: Process and Product.* Portsmouth, NH: Heinemann.

This book is a collection of articles whose authors have all used portfolios extensively in assessing student performance in writing. The articles contain sound justification for portfolio assessment and practical advice about starting a program. This book will be most helpful at the college and secondary levels. Ordering information: $20.00 from Heinemann Educational Books (see previous address).

Mitchell, R. (1992). *Testing for Learning: How New Approaches to Evaluation Can Improve American Schools.* New York: Free Press.

This book argues that schools must move from testing to assessment (using performances and portfolios). The book gives a good explanation of various aspects of assessment and includes specific examples of alternative assessment being done in various parts of the country and at various grade levels. Ordering information: $19.95 from Macmillan Publishing, Front & Brown Sts., Riverside, NJ 08375.

National Council of Teachers of English. (1992). *English Journal,* 81(2).

Several articles in this issue are on portfolios. Although all are based on use in the English classroom, they provide information that would be useful for the integration of portfolios into other subjects as well. Ordering information: Subscriptions are a part of the $40.00/year membership fee for individuals or institutions. Single copies are $6.00. Order from National Council of Teachers of English, 1111 Kenyon Rd., Urbana, IL 61801.

Perrone, V. (ed.). (1991). *Expanding Student Assessment.* Alexandria, VA: Association for Supervision and Curriculum Development.

This collection of articles on assessment is intended to expand understanding of the goals of assessment and introduce assessment alternatives that can be used throughout the curriculum. Ordering information: $14.95 from Association for Supervision and Curriculum Development (see previous address).

Phi Delta Kappa. (1989). *Phi Delta Kappan,* 70(9).

Most of the articles in this issue address testing—standardized and authentic—and authentic assessment in general. Ordering information: Subscriptions are $35.00/year. Single copies are $4.50. Order from Phi Delta Kappa, Eighth & Union, P.O. Box 789, Bloomington, IN 47402.

———. (1991). *Phi Delta Kappan,* 73(3).

Several articles in this issue address accountability and national, statewide, and standardized testing. Ordering information: Subscriptions are $35.00/year. Single copies are $4.50. Order from Phi Delta Kappa (see previous address).

Portfolio News.

This quarterly newsletter contains articles written by educators about using portfolios. Each issue also includes an annotated bibliography of literature about portfolios and a list of schools around the country using portfolios, with short descriptions of their programs. Ordering information: Subscriptions are $25.00/year. Order from Portfolio News: Subscriptions, Portfolio Assessment Clearinghouse, c/o San Dieguito Union High School District, 710 Encinitas Blvd., Encinitas, CA 92024.

Sizer, T. R. (1984). *Horace's Compromise: The Dilemma of the American High School.* Boston: Houghton Mifflin.

Sizer's "First Report of a Study of High Schools" includes the nine principles of effective schools from the Coalition of Essential Schools, with the good explanation "Diploma by Exhibition." Ordering information: $8.95 (pbk.) from Houghton Mifflin, 2 Park St., Boston, MA 02108.

————. (1992). *Horace's School.* Boston: Houghton Mifflin.

Theodore Sizer provides a blueprint for making American high schools places of thoughtfulness where students practice exhibiting the competencies and thought processes needed in the real world. Ordering information: $19.95 from Houghton Mifflin (see previous address).

Siggins, R. J., E. Rubel, and O. Edys. (1988). *Measuring Thinking Skills in the Classroom.* Washington, DC: National Education Association.

An inexpensive and useful work. Ordering information: $8.95 from NEA, P.O. Box 509, West Haven, CT 06516.

"This Is My Best": Vermont's Writing Assessment Program. (1991). Montpelier, VT: Vermont Department of Education.

This report presents information about Vermont's statewide writing-assessment program for grades 4 and 8, which piloted in 1990-91. Included are a specific description of the program (both theoretical and practical), an evaluation of the pilot-year results, and teacher reactions to the program. Ordering information: $5.00 from Vermont Department of Education, 120 State St., Montpelier, VT 05620.

Tierney, R. J., M. A. Carter, and L. E. Desai. (eds.). (1991). *Portfolio Assessment in the Reading-Writing Classroom.* Norwood, MA: Christopher-Gordon.

This book provides examples of teacher materials and student portfolios for different grades and subjects. The editors' stated purpose is to help teachers design classroom-assessment activities that are student-centered. Ordering information: $18.95 from Christopher-Gordon Publishers, 480 Washington St., Norwood, MA 02062.

The Moderate Level

At the moderate level, the library media specialist is more actively involved in the design of the instructional unit. The teacher and library media specialist co-plan the assessment. If the assessment will be in writing, the library media specialist offers use of library computers and instruction in word processing for those students who are not experienced. If the assessment is to involve production of audiovisual materials, the library media specialist assumes responsibility for teaching students production techniques and for helping students produce quality work. If the assessment is to be performance-based, the library media specialist offers to teach certain performance techniques such as how to make an oral presentation or how to present oneself on camera. The library media specialist also monitors preparations and rehearsals for certain performance groups while the teacher is involved in assessing the performances of other groups. The support of the library media specialist frees a teacher to try alternative assessment forms.

A SCENARIO

Joan Winter, a sixth-grade teacher, noticed that her students were oblivious to events happening in the real world. They read the *Weekly Reader*, but none of the news seemed to come alive. She approached the library media specialist, Valerie Brummer, with her concern.

Joan: I'm looking for a way to get my students involved with what's happening in the world. They don't seem to care about the environment or wars or even people in other places.

Valerie: We can get some real current information electronically. What have you thought they might do with the information?

Joan: I don't know. They think that reports are boring.

Valerie: Why don't we have them do their own *Weekly Reader* with a mixture of national, international, and school news?

Joan: I think they'd like that, but I don't know how I'd get it done. They wouldn't know where to start. And I don't think I have the time anyway.

Valerie: Let's use the current *Weekly Reader* as a model. We'll let the students take it apart and look at how each section is done. They can decide which sections to continue and which sections to add. As for the time, let's make this a joint project with the library. I can work with them during library time to collect information and write stories. We have a wonderful computer program that will help them lay out the news magazine.

Joan: Oh, that sounds great! You know, I don't want this to be a one-time project. I think they'll get a lot better as the year goes on. I'd like to give them a chance to improve.

Valerie: Why don't we start portfolios for each of the students? We've been talking about trying that anyway. Then we can let the students collect their best stories throughout the year. By the end of the year, the students will be able to see their own progress.

Joan: Yes, I think this unit is going to be exactly what the students need to get them excited about the world around them.

The In-Depth Level

Instructional Design Team Participation

At this level, the library media specialist helps the classroom teacher design the assessment strategies. In the previous scenario, in addition to suggesting the use of portfolios, the library media specialist would help formulate the goals for the portfolios based on a knowledge of students' experience with skills and content at other grade levels. Because library media specialists work with all students in the school, they offer teachers a global (whole-school) perspective.

Perhaps an even greater help to the teachers than designing the assessment strategies is a willingness on the part of the library media specialist to serve as an evaluator for student work. Because performance-based assessments should be evaluated by someone without a vested interest, the library media specialist helps the students and classroom teachers by filling that role whenever possible. Library media specialists also evaluate written student products, especially those based on research in the library.

In-Services

At this level of involvement, library media specialists provide in-service on authentic assessment strategies. This is especially valuable as teachers shift from traditional, rote-memory tests to more open-ended and authentic assessment techniques. Teachers need extensive in-service training to become comfortable with these new strategies. The library media specialist can become an expert in assessment and personally conduct the in-service sessions or can plan workshops in which a variety of materials are made available, teachers have the opportunity to work together, and guest speakers are invited to share their expertise.

REFERENCES

Brozo, W. G. (1990). Learning How At-Risk Readers Learn Best: A Case for Interactive Assessment. *Journal of Reading* 33(7), 522-527.

Chittenden, E. (1991). Authentic Assessment, Evaluation, and Documentation of Student Performance. In V. Perrone (ed.), *Expanding Student Assessment* (pp. 22-31). Alexandria, VA: Association for Supervision and Curriculum Development.

Diez, M. E., and C. J. Moon. (1992). What Do We Want Students to Know? . . . and Other Important Questions. *Educational Leadership,* 49(8), 38-41.

Herman, J. L. (1992). What Research Tells Us About Good Assessment. *Educational Leadership,* 49(8), 74-78.

Mehrens, W. A. (1992). Using Performance Assessment for Accountability Purposes. *Educational Measurement: Issues and Practice,* 11(1), 3-9.

Meyer, C. A. (1992). What's the Difference Between *Authentic* and *Performance* Assessment? *Educational Leadership,* 49(8), 39-40.

Murray, J. P. (1990). Better Testing for Better Learning. *College Teaching,* 38(4), 148-152.

Newmann, F. M. (1991). Linking Restructuring to Authentic Student Achievement. *Phi Delta Kappan,* 72(6), 458-463.

Paulson, F. L., P. R. Paulson, and C. A. Meyer. (1991). What Makes a Portfolio a Portfolio? *Educational Leadership,* 48(5), 60-63.

Perrone, V. (ed.). (1991). *Expanding Student Assessment.* Alexandria, VA: Association for Supervision and Curriculum Development.

Peters, C. W. (1991). You Can't Have Authentic Assessment Without Authentic Content. *Reading Teacher,* 44(8), 590-591.

Portfolio News. Published quarterly by Portfolio Assessment Clearinghouse, c/o San Dieguito Union High School District, 710 Encinitas Blvd., Encinitas, CA 92024.

Vavrus, L. (1990). Put Portfolios to the Test. *Instructor,* 100(1), 48-53.

Wiggins, G. (1989). A True Test: Toward More Authentic and Equitable Assessment. *Phi Delta Kappan,* 70(9), 703-713.

———. (1992). Creating Tests Worth Taking. *Educational Leadership,* 49(8), 26-33.

Zessoules, R., and H. Gardner. (1991). Authentic Assessment: Beyond the Buzzword and into the Classroom. In V. Perrone (ed.), *Expanding Student Assessment* (pp. 47-71). Alexandria, VA: Association for Supervision and Curriculum Development.

ADDITIONAL READINGS

Altieri, G. (1990). A Structural Model for Student Outcomes: Assessment Programs in Community Colleges. *Community College Review,* 17(4), 15-21.
Outlines a model program for a community college assessment program that measures student outcomes.

Archbald, D. A., and Newmann, F. M. (1988). *Beyond Standardized Testing: Assessing Authentic Academic Achievement in the Secondary School.* Reston, VA: National Association of Secondary School Principals.

Details three types of alternative assessment: tests of discrete competencies (language performance, analysis and problem solving, specific curriculum content); exhibitions; and portfolios and profiles. Offers guidelines for implementing assessment programs and investigates the continued use of standardized testing.

Ballard, L. (1992). Portfolios and Self-Assessment. *English Journal,* 81(2), 46-48.

Describes the positive effects of allowing students the opportunity (as their final) to assess their own writing and their progress in writing during the year.

Barone, T. (1991). Assessment as Theater: Staging an Exposition. *Educational Leadership,* 48(5), 57-59.

Describes an exposition in which students demonstrated through portfolios and performances their intellectual and emotional growth that occurred as a result of REACH, a South Carolina humanities program.

Christenson, S. L., and J. E. Ysseldyke. (1989). Assessing Student Performance: An Important Change Is Needed. *Journal of School Psychology,* 27(4), 409-425.

Suggests that assessment of student performance should be changed from simple description to a view that leads to intervening in and changing a student's instructional program.

Cizek, G. J. (1991). Innovation or Enervation? Performance Assessment in Perspective. *Phi Delta Kappan,* 72(9), 695-699.

Expresses the view that performance assessment is not a quick solution to assessment problems.

Cooper, W., and B. J. Brown. (1992). Using Portfolios to Empower Student Writers. *English Journal,* 81(2), 40-45.

Describes the components and the process of compiling portfolios for an English language-arts classroom.

Frazier, D. M., and F. L. Paulson. (1992). How Portfolios Motivate Reluctant Writers. *Educational Leadership,* 49(8), 62-65.

An elementary teacher documents success with personal-writing portfolios kept by her fourth-grade students and with classroom portfolios that demonstrate achievement of district goals by all the students.

Fuchs, L. S., and S. L. Deno. (1991). Paradigmatic Distinctions Between Instructionally Relevant Measurement Models. *Exceptional Children,* 57(6), 488-500.

Contrasts two assessment models—measurement of specific subskills versus measurement of curriculum-based general outcomes.

Hansen, J. (1992). Literacy Portfolios: Helping Students Know Themselves. *Educational Leadership,* 49(8), 66-68.

Demonstrates the effectiveness of literacy portfolios in helping students discover who they are and what is important to them.

Hebert, E. A. (1992). Portfolios Invite Reflection—From Students *and* Staff. *Educational Leadership,* 49(8), 58-61.

Provides a view of an elementary school faculty that has made the assessment process more meaningful by using a learning-experiences form that includes comments instead of grades and by letting students share their portfolios with parents during portfolio evenings.

Heshusius, L. (1991). Curriculum-Based Assessment and Direct Instruction: Critical Reflections on Fundamental Assumptions. *Exceptional Children,* 57(4), 315-328.

Argues that assessment should be based on the human processes of learning rather than on curriculum-based assessment (CBA) and direct instruction (DI).

Krechevsky, M. (1991). Project Spectrum: An Innovative Assessment Alternative. *Educational Leadership,* 48(5), 43-48.

Details the features and effectiveness of the Spectrum program, in which children are assessed based on their performance in a number of domains, allowing all children a variety of opportunities for success.

Maeroff, G. I. (1991). Assessing Alternative Assessment. *Phi Delta Kappan,* 73(4), 272-281.

Investigates alternative assessment techniques, offering comprehensive discussion of both strengths and weaknesses.

McLean, L. D. (1990). Time to Replace the Classroom Test with Authentic Measurement. *Alberta Journal of Educational Research,* 36(1), 78-84.

Argues that portfolios (systematic, cumulative records of performance) are very promising for authentically assessing student achievement.

Mitchell, R. (1992). *Testing for Learning: How New Approaches to Evaluation Can Improve American Schools.* New York: Free Press.

Explains various aspects of assessment and includes specific examples of alternative assessment being done by different schools.

O'Brien, C. W. (1992). A Large-Scale Assessment to Support the Process Paradigm. *English Journal,* 81(2), 28-33.

Describes a large-scale writing-assessment program based on a writing process approach that has been instituted successfully in Missouri.

O'Neil, J. (1992). Putting Performance Assessment to the Test. *Educational Leadership,* 49(8), 14-19.

Describes efforts by several states to replace traditional testing programs with performance-assessment plans (including both performances and portfolios).

Paris, S. G. (1991). Portfolio Assessment for Young Readers. *Reading Teacher,* 44(9), 680-682.
Describes portfolio assessments for children in the primary grades that engage the students in authentic learning and provide guidance for instruction.

Pickering, J. W., and J. C. Bowers. (1990). Assessing Value-Added Outcomes Assessment. *Measurement and Evaluation in Counseling and Development,* 22(4), 215-221.
Discusses and evaluates research on the value-added assessment model (in which students' knowledge at the end of school is measured against their knowledge at the beginning).

Portfolios Illuminate the Path for Dynamic, Interactive Readers. *Journal of Reading,* 33(8), 644-647.
Asserts that portfolios can improve students' self-esteem and confidence because they involve collaboration between teachers and students and they allow students to build on their strengths rather than focus on their weaknesses.

Shavelson, R. J., and G. P. Baxter. (1992). What We've Learned About Assessing Hands-On Science. *Educational Leadership,* 49(8), 20-25.
Details the characteristics of performance assessments that provide accurate measures of student achievement and improve the quality of teaching.

Stiggins, R. J. (1990). Toward a Relevant Classroom Assessment Research Agenda. *Alberta Journal of Educational Research,* 36(1), 92-97.
Provides perspectives on classroom assessment in the future and suggests that it will be improved when it is separated from high-stakes testing.

———. (1991). Assessment Literacy. *Phi Delta Kappan,* 72(7), 534-539.
Offers a convincing argument that educators and the public must focus research and development as well as teacher-training efforts on assessment literacy.

Stiggins, R. J., and N. F. Conklin. (1992). *In Teachers' Heads: Investigating the Practices of Classroom Assessment.* Albany, NY: State University of New York Press.
Very up-to-date treatment of a developing issue.

Stiggins, R. J., N. F. Conklin, and N. J. Bridgeford. (1986). Classroom Assessment: A Key to Effective Education. *Educational Measurement: Issues and Practice,* 5(2), 5-17.
Reviews the literature on assessment and concludes that classroom assessments will not be accepted by the measurement community until research and training in teacher-led classroom assessment is conducted.

Traub, R. E. (1990). Assessment in the Classroom: What Is the Role of Research? *Alberta Journal of Educational Research,* 36(1), 85-91.
Investigates the nature of classroom assessment and suggests further research that is needed in the area.

Wilson, R. J. (1990). Classroom Processes in Evaluating Student Achievement. *Alberta Journal of Educational Research,* 36(1), 4-17.

Reports research results demonstrating that evaluation of student achievement by the classroom teacher is often conducted simply as a summative exercise to generate grades rather than as a formative mode of feedback to help the teacher modify instruction.

Wolf, D. P., P. G. LeMahieu, and J. Eresh. (1992). Good Measure: Assessment as a Tool for Educational Reform. *Educational Leadership*, 49(8), 8-13.

Discusses the validity of using portfolios and exhibitions to encourage thoughtfulness among students, faculty, and parents and to provide reliable assessment of student achievement.

8

What's the Difference Between *Authentic* and *Performance* Assessment?

 Carol A. Meyer

Performance assessment and *authentic assessment* are often used interchangeably, but do they mean the same thing? Although both labels might appropriately apply to some types of assessment, they are not synonymous. We must be clear about the differences if we are to support each other in developing improved assessments.

TWO EXAMPLES

To distinguish between the two terms, let's look at a familiar form of assessment with which we have a wealth of experience. Following are two examples of a direct writing assessment in which students produce writing samples.

Case 1: Every May school district X conducts a direct writing assessment. For four days, all students at selected grade levels participate in a standardized series of activities to produce their writing samples. Using a carefully scripted manual, teachers guide students through the assessment with limited teacher directions and extended student writing time (up to 45 minutes) each day: Topic Introduction and Pre-writing (Day 1), Rough Drafting (Day 2), Revising and Editing (Day 3), and Final Copying and Proofreading (Day 4). The assessment clearly supports the Writing-as-a-Process instructional model.

Case 2: School district Y also conducts a direct writing assessment annually in May. Each student has a conference with his or her teacher to determine which paper from the student's portfolio to submit for assessment purposes. The papers in the portfolio have not been generated under standardized conditions but, rather, represent the ongoing work of the student for the year. All the papers were developed by the student, with as much or as little time allocated to each of the Writing-as-a-Process stages as he or she saw fit.

Is Case 1 an example of a performance assessment? Yes. The students are asked to perform specific behaviors that are to be assessed: to prove that they can write, the students produce a writing sample. Is Case 2 an example of a performance assessment? Yes, also. The portfolio contains numerous examples of actual student performance, although much of the structure associated with testing has been removed.

Reprinted from *Educational Leadership* 49, no. 8 (May 1992): pp. 39-41. Copyright 1992. Used with permission.

Is Case 1 an example of an authentic assessment? No. While the students are asked to perform the specific behavior to be assessed, the context is contrived. In real life, individuals seldom write under the conditions imposed during a standardized direct writing assessment. Is Case 2 an example of an authentic assessment? Yes. Performance is assessed in a context more like that encountered in real life; for example, students independently determined how long to spend on the various stages of the writing process, creating as many or as few rough drafts as they saw necessary to complete their final copies.

As we can see, performance assessment refers to the kind of student response to be examined; authentic assessment refers to the context in which that response is performed. While not all performance assessments are authentic, it is difficult to imagine an authentic assessment that would not also be a performance assessment.

CRITERIA FOR AUTHENTICITY

To determine whether a given performance assessment is authentic, we must ask, "Authentic to what?" It is a seemingly simple question, but one whose answer may be complex. The following are just a few facets of authenticity: stimuli, task complexity, locus of control, motivation, spontaneity, resources, conditions, criteria, standards, consequences.

Some of these points may be more critical than others in a particular assessment. The assessor needs to make that determination. But in labeling an assessment as authentic, the assessor must specify in what respects the assessment is authentic.

Moreover, because authenticity has a multidimensional nature, some assessments are more authentic than others. Ironically, the most authentic assessment in many situations can probably not be contrived for purposes of testing, for then it would no longer be totally authentic. Educators and assessors must thus be explicit about which facets of authenticity are most critical.

PROPOSED DEFINITIONS

Two definitions may help further clarify the distinction between the two terms.

In a performance assessment, the student completes or demonstrates the same behavior that the assessor desires to measure. There is a minimal degree, if any, of inference involved. For examples, if the behavior to be measured is writing, the student writes. The student does not complete multiple-choice questions about sentences and paragraphs, which instead measure the student's abilily to proofread other people's writing, and require a high degree of inference about the student's ability to write.

In an authentic assessment, the student not only completes or demonstrates the desired behavior, but also does it in a real-life context. "Real life" may be in terms of the student (for example, the classroom) or an adult expectation. The significant criterion for the authenticity of a writing assessment might be that the locus of control rests with the student; that is, the student determines the topic, the time allocated, the pacing, and the conditions under which the writing sample is generated.

IMPLICATIONS FOR EDUCATORS

What significance do these definitions have for educators? First, when we read materials or attend presentations, we must determine whether the authors or presenters are sensitive to the distinction between the two terms. We must be particularly cautious of generalizing from information provided by individuals who use the terms interchangeable.

Second, we must become informed consumers when purchasing tests, assessment programs, or other materials being marketed as either performance or authentic assessments. Buzzwords sell, unfortunately, so beware.

Third, when planning an assessment, we must carefully identify the purpose in order to determine whether performance assessment—authentic or not—is relevant. Only appropriate matches will improve assessment of student learning.

9

Practicing Authentic
Assessment in
the School Library

 BARBARA K. STRIPLING

*October 12, 1992. The auxiliary gym in a medium-size high school brims with
library study carrels, almost unrecognizable behind the posters, realia, and fact
sheets on display. Buzzing around each booth are fourth-, fifth-, and sixth-
graders eagerly listening to high school students teaching about the days of
Columbus and the legacy that resulted for today's Americans. At the disease and
medicine booth, 10 fourth-graders line up as Native Americans. Nine of them are
marked with red spots and instructed to fall dead to the gym floor (from smallpox
and measles). The remaining Native American looks around for support when
Columbus's men start making demands, but he is alone and powerless. Across
the gym at the food booth, a plate of live worms (grubs), potatoes, and tomatoes
is on display while the students talk about which foods went from the Americas
to Europe and which foods came from the other direction. The students include
the effect that the exchange of foods had on each culture. At the art booth, students
see videodisc images of art from the late 1400s, compare those paintings with
modern abstract art, and have a chance to create their own art in whichever style
they choose.*

"We were great!" "When can we do something like that again?" "I didn't know
it was so much fun to teach." Seventy at-risk high school students patted themselves
on the back after our successful Days of Columbus Fair. Four teachers nodded and
smiled at the power of authentic assessment, remembering, however, that the
journey to October 12 echoed Columbus's voyage itself. We had picked a destina-
tion, but we were not certain how to get there, what maelstroms we would face along
the way, or what it would look like once we finished the travel (travail). Despite the
uncertainties, the world we discovered through authentic assessment has forever
changed our instructional strategies.

Reprinted from *School Library Media Annual, 1993* (pp. 40-55) by Carol Collier Kuhlthau, ed.
Englewood, CO: Libraries Unlimited. Copyright 1993. Used with permission.

CHARACTERISTICS OF AUTHENTIC ASSESSMENT

Authentic assessment is not a new concept in education. For years, students in auto mechanics have been asked to demonstrate that they can repair a car motor, students in drama have been producing plays, and students in athletics have competed in athletic contests. A faulty car motor is a real-life problem. Students have to apply what they have learned to figure out the problem and fix it; they must think during the assessment process (and assessment is a continuous process, not an I'll-see-what-you-know-on-Tuesday, one-shot chance). The students stop at various stages in their repair process to discuss with their teacher and with each other how well their repairs are going. Students continue their work until they decide they have been successful; they do not settle for a 65 percent repaired engine. Repairing a car motor is authentic assessment because it is a learning experience in itself, put into a real-life context and based on authentic content. The student is doing the thinking and the work. The assessment is ongoing, and it involves reflection by the teacher and student.

A key to authentic assessment is authentic content, defined as important concepts that are consistent with local, state, and national curriculum guidelines and applicable to the real world. Car repair can be easily identified as authentic vocational content; in academic subject areas, however, the connections to real life are more abstract. National professional organizations in mathematics, science, English, and social studies have issued major curriculum documents within the past three years to define the important concepts in those subject areas (see appendix 9.A on page 119 for a description of these documents). These K-12 documents provide a content framework that builds on prior knowledge and the developmental level of the students. The individual teacher's ingenuity must connect the content within the frameworks to real-life experiences that require a high level of thinking from the students. That connection leads to authentic content.

IMPETUS FOR AUTHENTIC ASSESSMENT

The nationwide struggle to improve education, referred to variously as restructuring, transforming education, or essential schools has led naturally to a new emphasis on authentic assessment. The principles that underlie many successful efforts to change schools have been expressed by Theodore Sizer and the Coalition of Essential Schools in their "Nine Common Principles of Essential Schools."[1] These guidelines not only make intuitive sense, they work. Teachers are asked to be generalists first and to focus on helping all students learn to use their minds well. The curriculum is concentrated in fewer areas, allowing students and teachers to pursue content in depth rather than breadth.

Students are expected to become personally involved with the learning and to assume responsibility for their own learning with their teachers serving as facilitators. Furthermore, students are expected to demonstrate their learning, necessitating alternative assessment methods.

The atmosphere in an essential school is personalized and nonthreatening. Teachers and students work cooperatively, classes are small, and the school structure is flexible enough to allow for personalization and collaboration.

Sizer has declared that a school must be a place of thoughtfulness.[2] Howard Gardner believes schools should "inculcate in their students the highest degree of understanding."[3] Both want schools to move beyond basic skills and rote memory; they expect students to understand and apply what they learn in school to real-life situations. Sizer has even suggested a curriculum structure for engendering thoughtfulness. He envisions the curricular areas of history/philosophy, the arts (including foreign languages and literature), and science/math surrounding a core of essential skills of inquiry and expression that include thoughtfulness, organization, thinking/reflection, study skills, and communication.[4] School library media specialists recognize that the core also includes information skills. In fact, Sizer himself has recognized the central role of school libraries: "Not surprisingly, one good way to start designing an Essential school is to plan a library and let its shadow shape the rest"[5] (see fig. 9.1).

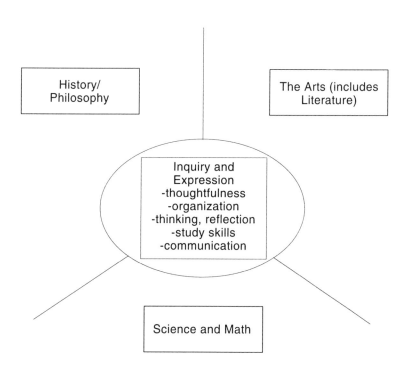

Fig. 9.1. Theodore Sizer's Model of a Restructured School.

If the primary goal of education is to cultivate thoughtfulness and understanding and if the school library media center is at the core of that effort, then school library media specialists must lead in changing assessment techniques from rote-memory, end-of-unit exams that are the standard in many schools. Instead, students must be expected to work through a thoughtful process of building understandings. Assessment techniques must allow teachers and library media specialists to measure students' progress and their ability to apply their understandings to new situations.

TYPES OF AUTHENTIC ASSESSMENT

Alternative assessment techniques that fulfill the principles of school reform include

- personal contact through observations and interviews,
- performances and exhibitions,
- portfolios, and
- authentic tests.

Personal-contact assessment can be between teacher and student, student and student, or teacher and groups of students. Contact can be formal or informal and can serve to evaluate progress, pinpoint frustrations, redirect activities, provide nurturing, or cause the student to self-assess. Personal contact usually results in a qualitative conversation; therefore, students are not worried about getting a specific grade, and they can be honest about where they are in the learning process. Because students will be honest with each other, peer contact is especially helpful during the process of learning.

Performances and exhibitions are closely related. A performance involves a prepared demonstration of learning such as performing a play, making an oral presentation, or participating in a debate. During an exhibition, either students can present a learning product they have already prepared or they can be asked to react to a new situation, applying what they have learned. In both instances, students discuss and defend the learning product with an evaluation panel. Exhibition products can include a performance, a solution to a problem, a portfolio, or any product that involves creativity, reflective thinking, and application of understandings to a new situation.

Portfolios can be approached in a number of ways. For most portfolio advocates, a portfolio is not simply a collection of student work. Students set learning goals (consistent with the teacher's goals), decide which pieces best demonstrate competence in those goals, revise those pieces using peer and teacher input, prepare a written reflection on the success of each piece included, and write an introduction that synthesizes their learning through the whole portfolio.

Gardner advocates a slightly different approach to portfolios—process-folios. Process-folios are appropriate for major projects. The folios include initial brainstorming, early drafts and critiques, journal entries of critical moments when new understandings are reached, works by others that particularly inspired or influenced the project, interim and final drafts, self-assessment, assessment by others (including peers, teachers, outside experts), and suggestions about directions the project can take in the future.[6]

Authentic tests involve application of previous learning to new, real-world situations or problems. The tests are learning situations in themselves. Therefore, a test that asks a student simply to remember and repeat previously learned information would not be authentic. Many teachers find that authentic tests are difficult to create and evaluate.

MOTIVATING WITH AUTHENTIC ASSESSMENT

Authentic assessment is a real boon to school library media centers. Just as the restructuring movement designates libraries as an essential center of the school's curriculum, the assessment trend leads teachers and students to projects and in-depth work that often can best be completed with a media center available and with the facilitation of the library media specialist.

In terms of student learning, authentic assessment affects two main areas: motivation and thinking skills. The Days of Columbus Fair offers a case study on motivation, although similar effects have been shown when students produce class magazines, letters to the editor, videotaped programs to be shown to other classes, or other projects. The 70 students who produced the fair are in a multidisciplinary (English, world history, economics) class called Connections. They are the battered ones, the students who get lost in a regular classroom, who cry out to be recognized as individuals, but often in socially unacceptable ways. Probably not one of the 70 has ever previously completed a library research project and enjoyed it. But the authenticity of the fair caught their enthusiasm. Students were allowed to choose their topic to study in depth and were grouped according to their choices. They decided how to pursue their topic and how to divide the work among group members. Both their research and the preparation of their booths were geared to appeal to a real audience—students from a nearby elementary school.

The Connections students exercised care and creativity in producing booths they could use to teach the history and legacy of their subject in ways that were understood and appreciated by their young fans. Pencils were given away at the invention booth because graphite was discovered in 1492; elementary students were given clay to create gods like the Aztec sculptures Columbus's men discovered; students were taught to play an Aztec forerunner of hacky sack; samples of fruit discovered in the new world were eagerly devoured (except the pomegranates, which most students had never seen).

As a part of the unit, the Connections students were involved in peer and self-assessment. They were asked to evaluate their own booth and the participation of each group member. They also were asked to evaluate two other booths and offer helpful suggestions to their classmates. Then they evaluated the success of the unit as a whole, including their research time in the library. Sixty-eight non-research-oriented students had positive things to say about their research time in the library! And the students are clamoring for another project like the fair. That's 68 testimonials to the motivating power of authentic assessment.

INCREASING THINKING
SKILLS WITH
AUTHENTIC ASSESSMENT

Reflection

Authentic assessment can also be powerful in raising the level of students' thinking. Built in to authentic assessment is one technique that has been proven effective at increasing thoughtfulness—periodic reflection. Reflection is particularly valuable in the library media center, where students can be lost in the stacks (or research process) for a couple of days before either the student or the teacher realizes the lack of focus. Several variations of reflection can easily be used within the context of library research.

Learning Logs

Learning logs are a way of building reflection into the note-taking process. The student sets up a two-column note sheet, using the left column for the notes and the right for reactions to the notes. Learning logs can be used any time a student is responsible for writing down information (from library sources, interviews, lecture notes, notes about research processes). The purpose of a learning log is to help students learn to interact mentally and emotionally with their notes. Not only do they learn more while they are taking notes but they also become more personally involved with their subject. Reactions can include personal comments or feelings about the information ("I think companies that dump toxic waste should be heavily fined"); questions ("What are the laws on toxic-waste dumping?"); notes about organization ("Use this in intro"); connections to previous knowledge ("Toxic-waste dumping is worse than oil spills because it's intentional").

Progress Logs

Students use progress logs to reflect on their success in finding appropriate information. They are asked to think about the ideas they are gathering in order to fit them into a framework of ideas or to figure out new directions to pursue.

Students can reflect on their own progress in understanding through a variety of techniques:

- Encapsulation: Students briefly note the main understanding they gathered that day (on a 3-x-5-inch card, for example).

- Research log: Students keep a research log during their whole process of research. Each day they set a goal. At the end of the period, students write what they accomplished during that day and what problems or frustrations they had. The library media specialist responds with specific suggestions or general encouragement.

- Conferencing/oral reflection: Library media specialists help students reflect on their daily progress by conferencing with individuals during the period or by calling the students together toward the end of the period to share their reflections orally.

- Reflection to a peer: Students take advantage of peer help by sharing their progress with a peer, who records the information for sharing with the library media specialist or teacher.

- Simplified outline: Students create a simplified visual or verbal outline at several points during their research. Such an outline should help them see where their information is confusing or scarce.

- Visualization: Students design graphics or visualizations to portray the important points about their subject. Visualizing helps students clarify what they think and feel about the topic.

Process Logs

Interspersed with supervising progress logs, library media specialists can direct students to think about their processes of finding information. Students need to reflect on their information processes (their research, thinking, and study skills) during a research unit and keep written records using various process-log techniques.

- Reflection points: Reflection points built into the research process challenge students to stop and ask themselves some questions at various points during their research.[7] Depending on the answers, the students either proceed or go back to fill in a missing part of the process.

- Process reflection: Students may use any of the previously mentioned techniques (encapsulation, daily log, oral sharing, peer sharing, simplified outline, visualization) to reflect on what they have learned about how to do research effectively. The library media specialist can vary the prompts so that students reflect on content one day and on process the next. (Content: "What is the most interesting new idea you discovered today? How does it help you answer one of your research questions?"; Process: "What material have you found in the reference collection? What process did you use to find it? If you found nothing in reference, where did you hit a dead end?")

Thoughtful Research Products

Library media specialists can combine the authentic-assessment effects of motivation and increased thinking skills by working with teachers to develop creative product ideas. A structure that helps teachers and library media specialists pinpoint thinking levels and gradually work students to higher levels is REACTS: A Taxonomy of Research Reactions.[8] By using this taxonomy and adapting or adopting the example assignments, the library media specialist can offer teachers a variety of thoughtful reactions to research at six thinking levels. Creative products fulfill the criteria for authentic assessment and can be included as part of a student's portfolio or exhibition.

Level 1: Recalling

Students recall and report the main facts discovered. They make no attempt to analyze the information or reorganize it for comparison purposes. Following are example assignments:

- *Select* 5-10 accomplishments of the person you have researched. Produce a "Hall of Fame" poster with your biographee's photocopied picture and list of accomplishments. (Alternative: "Hall of Shame" poster.)

- After your class adopts a second- or third-grade class, write a letter to your assigned student *recounting* five interesting facts you discovered in your research.

- *List* five dos and don'ts about a social or health issue that you have researched.

- *Find* facts about your subject for each category determined by the class. Contribute your facts to a class electronic database.

- *Select* pictures about your researched subject from discarded magazines or make photocopied pictures; combine those pictures with text excerpts to construct a billboard featuring your subject.

- *Arrange* words important to your research in a crossword puzzle or word search for your classmates to solve.

- Write a letter to a friend *recalling* the information you gathered.

- *Identify* five facts about your subject that are particularly interesting. Put each on an index card. The cards will be used as the facts for a class Jeopardy game. Exchange the game with another class.

Level 2: Explaining

Students recall and restate, summarize, or paraphrase information. They find examples, explain events or actions. Students understand the information well enough to be able to put it in a new context. Following are example assignments:

- *Dramatize* a particularly exciting event associated with your research in an on-the-spot report.

- *Illustrate* important features about your research in a mobile.

- Write and *present* a "You Are There" news program about a particular event or person you researched.

- Keep a journal in which you *present* your reactions, thoughts, and feelings about your researched subject.

- *Show* the events of your research on a map and explain the importance of each event.

- Cut out newspaper ads that would have interested a historical figure you have researched. *Explain* their importance to the historical figure.

- *Demonstrate* the character and personality of a historical person by filling a paper bag with modern objects that reveal the major facets of the person's character.

- *Prepare* a job application or resume for a person you have researched.

- *Propose* a party with three celebrities invited to honor the person you have researched. *Describe* the menu and activities and explain why you chose those items.

- Keep an explorer's log book to *express* your impressions as you investigate the sights and way of life in another country through research.

Level 3: Analyzing

Students break a subject into its component parts (causes, effects, problems, solutions) and compare one part with another. Following are example assignments:

- Create a timeline for the events that led up to the situation you researched. *Correlate* social, political, religious, educational, and technological events.

- *Transplant* an event or famous person from one time period, country, or ecological system to another time or place. Explain the changes that would occur.

- *Construct* a carefully organized poster to examine a social issue.

- *Characterize* your researched historical person in an obituary that makes clear his or her role in the conflicts of the day.

- *Reconstruct* the personality and career of a person you have researched and play the role of that person in a "What's My Line?" game.

- Cast a film version of the event you researched. The characters could be *represented* by actors working today or classmates. Explain your choices carefully.

- *Compare* your life-style and neighborhood to those of people living in the time you have researched.

- Write a letter to the editor *scrutinizing* a local issue. Support your opinions with specific details from your research.

- *Rewrite* a historical event from two different points of view.

- Write a recipe for a historical event by researching, *analyzing* to pick out the main ingredients, and listing them in order with mixing instructions.

- *Organize* and create a travel brochure to attract visitors to the place or time period you have researched. Include all information that one would need to know plus fascinating details that would draw visitors.

Level 4: Challenging

Students make critical judgments about their subject based on internal or external standards. (Standards may be student's own, or teacher or class may decide criteria. "I didn't like it" or "I don't believe it" are not enough.) Following are example assignments:

- Produce a *critical* review (of a book, movie, or play) that can be printed in a local paper or aired on local television or radio stations.

- Act as an attorney and *argue* to punish or acquit a historical character or a country for a crime or misdeed.

- *Determine* as a movie producer whether to make a film of an actual historical event, with justification for the decision.

- *Defend* your judgment that a research subject (if it is an invention, machine, or some other item) should be placed in a time capsule to be dug up in 100 years.

- *Justify* the punishment or nonpunishment of a historical villain.

- *Judge* the merits of a researched subject by conducting a mock trial.

- *Debate* the issues of a controversial research topic with a classmate who researched the same topic.

- *Evaluate* the accuracy of a historical or teen-problem novel by comparing the "factual" information in the novel with the facts you discover through research. *Refute* the nonfactual information in a letter from "Dear Abby."

- *Investigate* a social or ecological problem. Prepare a report card on the issue that assigns a grade for each proposed or attempted solution (look at the cost, feasibility, probable success, ease of implementation). *Justify* your grades.

- Using a job evaluation form, *rate* a historical person's performance of his or her job based on your research. Justify your ratings.

- Create an editorial cartoon about your researched subject that makes clear your *judgment* about the subject.

Level 5: Transforming

Students bring together more than one piece of information, form their own conclusions, and present those conclusions in a creative new format. Following are example assignments:

- *Design* and *produce* a television commercial or a whole advertising campaign that presents your research results to the class.

- *Create* a board game that incorporates the major conclusions you reached about your researched subject.

- Write a poem or short story that *expresses* your new knowledge or insight.

- *Dramatize* a famous historical event. The dramatization should make clear your interpretation of the event.

- *Predict* your reaction to your research subject as a resident of the future.

- *Compose* a speech that a historical person might deliver about a present-day situation.

- Become a person in the historical era you have researched; *elaborate* from that perspective about a specific event, problem, invention, or fad in a letter to someone.

- *Predict* what your researched person would take on a trip. *Design* the itinerary. Pack that person's suitcase and present each item to the class with an explanation of its significance.

- Research a specific event, person, or aspect of the culture of a historical era. Write and *produce* a segment for a morning news show on your topic.

- *Pretend* that you are living in a particular historical era. Research a subject that was important during that era and write a newspaper or magazine article about that subject as though you were writing at that time. Work with your classmates to produce the entire newspaper or magazine.

- *Predict* what will happen with your researched subject in 50 years. Write a movie treatment for a science fiction movie that shows your predictions.

- *Design* a hypermedia program about your researched subject that allows others to follow several different paths through your information.

Level 6: Synthesizing

Students create an entirely original product based on a new concept or theory. Following are example assignments:

- *Develop* a model program to address a social problem that you have researched.

- *Invent* a new animal; explain its effect on other animals and on the environment.

- *Create* a new country and hypothesize about the change in the balance of power in the world.

- *Design* a new building, machine, process, experiment based on theories developed from your research.

- *Develop* proposed legislation to address national, state, or local issues.

- *Devise* an ethical code for present-day researchers or scientists that could regulate their activities in a particular field.

- *Develop* a community project that addresses an issue of local concern.

- *Design* and carry out a science project that builds on the previous knowledge that you have discovered through research and tests a new concept or theory.

- *Propose* an ethical code for political campaigning, keeping in mind the realities and the myths underlying politics.

ROLES OF THE LIBRARY MEDIA SPECIALIST IN AUTHENTIC ASSESSMENT

Catalyst for Change

The library media specialist is in an ideal position in the school to help teachers shift from textbook-based exams to alternative assessment techniques like projects, portfolios, and exhibitions. Library resources will be required for these assessments, and students will need sophisticated information skills to complete them. By coplanning with teachers, offering product alternatives, and teaching information literacy skills, library media specialists can provide both support and incentives for teachers to change their assessment techniques.

Facilitator of Learning

The restructured-school role of the teacher as a facilitator of students' learning is already comfortable and familiar for most library media specialists. Students working on library projects have always been held responsible for their own learning while being guided by the library media specialist.

With the authentic-assessment emphasis on higher levels of thinking, however, library media specialists may want to expand their facilitator role by adopting a six-step process shown by researchers to be effective in teaching for higher-level thinking.[9]

Step 1: Conduct preinstructional activities.

Step 2: Model the process.

Step 3: Guide student practice.

Step 4: Give checklists for evaluation.

Step 5: Provide for independent practice with new examples.

Step 6: Provide opportunity for application to new situation.

This process can be illustrated with a case study of a library unit to facilitate higher-level thinking and involving advanced sophomore English students. In this unit, the students must select individual topics within the broad subject of media. The emphasis in this project is on a thoughtful research process; therefore, the students' products are the process pieces (selection of topic, high-level thesis statement, analytical research questions, notes answering their questions, bibliography, and outline) rather than a final paper.

Ms. Grant, the advanced sophomore English teacher, glides into the library media center early for her appointment with the library media specialist, Ms. Easterly. At a break in the action, Ms. Easterly joins Ms. Grant at the table. After an initial discussion about the unit, they ask themselves some questions. Do the students already understand the concepts of a taxonomy and of levels of thinking? Have they ever been asked to write a thoughtful thesis statement before? What resources would help the students get overviews of media so that they know enough to write a tentative thesis? Once decisions have been made about students' prior knowledge, Ms. Grant and Ms. Easterly plan the scaffolds that will help students perform steps of the research assignment that they have not practiced before. Ms. Easterly finds moments during the next couple of days to develop the scaffolds—a model thesis and questions, a template for note-taking by question, and a sample bibliography. She also puts the best media overview books on reserve. [Step 1, preinstructional activities: Decide what students are ready to learn, develop scaffolds to help them, and select appropriate materials.]

The students arrive in the library and are greeted by a packet of cutouts: pictures of a musical note, a line of music, a musical score, a compact disc, and an advertisement for a recording studio with all its stars featured. They are asked to work in groups to put these objects in levels of increasing complexity. They talk about their arrangement, of course, but the real second step in the teaching-for-thinking process occurs when the students are asked to model their thinking for the other students. Each group explains how they made the choices they did. [Step 2, model the process: Use thinking aloud and precorrect anticipated student difficulties.]

Ms. Easterly draws from the students the characteristics of a taxonomy and then begins to explain Benjamin Bloom's taxonomy of the cognitive domain. As each level is explained, the students practice constructing a statement about media at that level of thinking. Thomas suggests a knowledge-level statement: "Television commercials for the Super Bowl cost up to $1 million for 30 seconds." Kerry offers an evaluation-level statement: "Violence in television cartooning is dangerous to small children because it convinces them that weapons are toys and that no one is killed forever." Ms. Easterly guides the students' suggestions until the class is comfortable with the statement at each thinking level.

Students are then asked to work in small groups to write tentative thesis statements (about teenagers) at the analysis, synthesis, and evaluation levels and to formulate questions that would have to be answered in order to prove the thesis statements. As statements and questions are shared with the whole class, students are asked to clarify and explain their thinking. [Step 3, guide students as they practice with new examples.]

Once the class has discussed the groups' efforts, Ms. Easterly gives each group a checklist of questions for assessing their own group's statements and questions. [Step 4, give students checklists to evaluate their work.]

(Case study continues on page 116.)

> *The sophomores are given the next couple of days to browse the overview books before they are asked to write a tentative thesis and analytical questions for their own media topic. The students dig in and decide on topics ranging from computer networking to Nazi propaganda. Amazingly, the sophomores do write thoughtful thesis statements and analytical questions using the handout provided by Ms. Easterly as a guide. At the project's end, Ms. Grant and Ms. Easterly are pleasantly surprised at how many students' notes match the thoughtfulness of their questions. Many of these students have been boosted to higher levels of thinking during research.* [Step 5, provide opportunity for independent practice using new examples.]
>
> *Of course the final step is for students to be able to apply their processes and thinking skills to totally new situations. Anytime these media-project students are asked to begin a research assignment, they should be able to construct a thoughtful, working thesis and analytical questions. They should also be able to take appropriate notes to answer their questions. This application step is, indeed, the goal of every library media specialist—for students to learn an information-search process that will work in any situation for the rest of their lives.* [Step 6, students apply their learning to entirely new situations.]

Evaluator of Process and Product

The third role for library media specialists in authentic assessment is that of evaluator, both of the units themselves and of the students' products. The unit evaluation can be formal or informal, but it should assess the effectiveness of the unit in motivating students to learn and in challenging them to think.

Unit evaluation must be shared among students, teachers, and the library media specialist just as learning in a restructured school is a shared responsibility. Reflection techniques used with students during the unit provide in-process evaluation. The library media specialist and the teacher must also grant themselves time during the unit for reflection. One effective technique is to write daily in a research log. If problems or frustrations are identified, small adjustments can be made during the unit.

The final evaluation of the unit builds on the earlier reflections. Because the teacher and library media specialist have a vested interest in the success of the unit, comments from students about where the unit succeeded and where it needed improvement may prove to be more insightful. Often student comments confirm opinions already formulated by the teacher and library media specialist.

Evaluating students' authentic-assessment products also offers the library media specialist valuable opportunities to influence student learning. Experts have said that exhibitions, performances, and portfolios are best evaluated by someone other than the classroom teacher; therefore, teachers are turning to evaluation panels of other classroom teachers, the library media specialist, administrators, parents, community members, and students. Because the evaluation must be consistent from student to student (even if the evaluators change from day to day), teachers and library media specialists can construct measuring instruments that describe the desired outcomes very precisely. The following categories can be used as a basis for descriptive statements:

Framework
- clarity of goals
- achievement of goals
- organization

Reflection (especially important for portfolios and exhibitions)
- students' assessments of their own progress
- depth of thought in reflective statements

Content
- comparison of content of each piece to standard of excellence
- thoughtfulness

Style
- originality, creativity
- voice

Presentation
- fluency
- overall appearance

A descriptive statement about "voice" might read: "The student has formed an evident personal connection to the subject." Evaluators would be asked to rate the students' performances on the voice statement using a five-point scale (1 = outstanding; 5 = unsatisfactory). The evaluation instrument contains statements on those items most important for each product, not on all the items just listed.

Because authentic-assessment instruments can be used consistently by different evaluators, the library media specialist is free to participate according to the demands of the library schedule. On some units, the library media specialist might be able to evaluate every student product; on others, maybe just a few. As long as the evaluation instrument is clear, the library media specialist is not restricted to evaluating only library research products. Students will appreciate the library media specialist's interest in all their learning activities.

CONCLUSION

Authentic assessment offers many opportunities for teachers and library media specialists to raise the level of students' interest in learning. Students enjoy seeing the connections of their learning to the real world. They are proud to create original products that they can share in situations beyond their classroom. Authentic assessment provides motivation and a spark of fun in learning, but the overwhelming implication of authentic assessment is that it helps students develop new understandings about their world.

NOTES

1.   Theodore R. Sizer, *Horace's School: Redesigning the American High School* (Boston: Houghton Mifflin, 1992), 207-9.

2.   Ibid., 128.

3.   Howard Gardner, *The Unschooled Mind: How Children Think and How Schools Should Teach* (New York: Basic Books, 1991), 18.

4.   Sizer, *Horace's School*, 151-57.

5.   Ted Sizer, "Colleagues and Conversation," *The Conversation* (September 1990). This is a Re:Learning newsletter published jointly by the Coalition of Essential Schools and the Education Commission of the States. In the same article, Sizer says: "If students are to be the 'workers' they absolutely require richly endowed libraries and the time to use them."

6.   Gardner., *The Unschooled Mind*, 240.

7.   For a fuller description of reflection points, see Barbara K. Stripling and Judy M. Pitts, *Brainstorms and Blueprints* (Englewood, CO: Libraries Unlimited, 1988), 59-60, 74, 87, 101, 120, 132, 142.

8.   Ibid., 8-18.

9.   Barak Rosenshine and Joseph Guenther, "Using Scaffolds for Teaching Higher Level Cognitive Strategies," in *Teaching for Thinking* (Reston, VA: National Association of Secondary School Principals, 1992), 37-44.

APPENDIX 9.A
CURRICULUM DOCUMENTS

JUDY M. PITTS

Charting a Course: Social Studies for the 21st Century. Washington, DC: National
    Commission on the Social Studies, 1989.

This document is the report of the Curriculum Task Force of the National
Commission on the Social Studies, a coalition of social studies educators and
university scholars. It sets forth goals and priorities for social studies education in
elementary and secondary schools. It includes a recommended curriculum for grades
K-12 as well as perspectives from specific social science associations such as those
interested in economics, political science, and sociology.

Curriculum and Evaluation Standards for School Mathematics. Reston, VA: Na-
    tional Council of Teachers of Mathematics, 1989.

These standards were developed by the Commission on Standards for School
Mathematics, a group appointed by the National Council of Teachers of Mathematics. The document presents a "coherent vision of what it means to be mathematically
literate" and a "set of standards to guide the revision of the school mathematics
curriculum and its associated evaluation toward this vision" (1). Goals are presented
for grades K-12. A special section on evaluation follows the goals. Each section also
includes a set of sample student activities that grow out of problem situations and
encourage active learning.

Everybody Counts: A Report to the Nation on the Future of Mathematics Education.
    Washington, DC: National Academy Press, 1989.

This report examines U.S. mathematics and science education from kindergarten through graduate school. It discusses curricula, teaching, and assessment and
charts a general course for the future. The report was prepared by the National
Research Council, which is made up of representatives from the National Academy
of Science, the National Academy of Engineering, and the Institute of Medicine.

Laughlin, M. A., H. M. Hartoonian, and N. M. Sanders. *From Information to*
    Decision Making: New Challenges for Effective Citizenship. Washington, DC:
    National Council for the Social Studies, 1989.

"This bulletin examines ways educators perceive the Information Age and react
to it" (1). It provides "readers with some ideas about ways social studies teachers
may become effective teachers in an Information Age" (vii). Specific lessons
dealing with information topics and ranging from grades K-12 are presented.
Chapter 9 by Daniel Callison is titled "School Media Programs in the Information
Age."

Lloyd-Jones, R., and A. A. Lunsford, eds. *The English Coalition Conference: Democracy Through Language.* Urbana, IL: National Council of Teachers of English, 1989.

This document presents the major conclusions reached at a conference sponsored by eight professional associations concerned with the teaching of English. It addresses concerns of and challenges to units teachers of English from kindergarten through graduate school. The conference theme, democracy through language, emerged to express participants' beliefs in the "value of English studies in the education of citizens who live in a democratic and increasingly complex information society" (xx).

Rutherford, F. J., and A. Ahlgren. *Science for All Americans.* New York: Oxford University Press, 1989.

This volume is the culmination of phase 1 of Project 2061, "a long-range, multiphase effort designed to help the nation achieve scientific literacy." The project was initiated by the American Association for the Advancement of Science. *Science for All Americans* establishes "a conceptual base for reform by defining the knowledge, skills, and attitudes all students should acquire as a consequence of their total school experience, from kindergarten through high school" (204).

Science for All Americans: Summary. Washington, DC: American Association for the Advancement of Science, 1989.

This summary of *Science for All Americans* introduces readers to Project 2061 and to the conceptual base presented fully in *Science for All Americans.*

10

The Potential for Portfolio Assessment

 DANIEL CALLISON

The term *portfolio* normally brings to mind a collection of stocks, examples of best art pieces, or a sample of wares to give tangible evidence of value, performance, and potential. The portfolio assessment technique is receiving an increasing amount of attention in the language arts and sciences as an option or as an addition to standardized tests. Portfolios offer the opportunity, when correctly used, to assess additional talents and abilities of students beyond the skills tested through multiple-choice responses.

With selected samples of student work gathered over time, a map of change, hopefully a record of progress, can be seen. The exact measures of that change are in discussion, not likely to be settled by a specific formula. Most proponents of the portfolio technique emphasize its strength for assessing student performance in terms of intellectual growth and maturity, higher conversation levels, self-assessment or goal setting, and depth of understanding. Although levels of development are often identified for measurement of progress, assessment is often made against the student's own record and not tied to any specific age or grade level.

Mapping for the purpose of assessment is not a new concept to school library media specialists. Over the past several years, methods in collection mapping, curriculum mapping, and planning or policy development have appeared in the literature. More and more school library media specialists are practicing some aspect of maintaining records related to collection and curriculum in order to visualize options and make decisions. Not only is such a process healthy for media specialists because they begin to think about goals and objectives in a very concrete manner, but such mapping leads to visual products that can be used to convey to others what changes are needed. Such mapping, analysis, documentation, and presentation become key elements for those school library media specialists who want to clearly define their educational roles both for their own professional growth and for others who must place a value on the school library media center program.

Reprinted from *School Library Media Annual, 1993* (pp. 30-39) by Carol Collier Kuhlthau, ed. Englewood, CO: Libraries Unlimited. Copyright 1993. Used with permission.

NEW CURRICULUM, NEW ASSESSMENT

Over the coming five years, those media specialists who desire a more specific role in student performance evaluation should give serious consideration to experimenting with the portfolio as a method to document the change in student reading, writing, and information use patterns. More important, however, is the probability that the portfolios will open new conversation levels between library media specialist and student, and between library media specialist and teacher or parent.

New curriculum designs in language arts and social studies lead to school library media programs that emphasize information literacy. The following instructional approaches move us beyond the standard test format and toward the broader assessment methods:

- an integration of all aspects of language arts including reading, writing, listening, and speaking;

- a focus on the process of constructing meaning;

- the use of literature that inspires and motivates readers;

- an emphasis on problem solving and higher-order thinking skills; and

- the use of collaboration and group work as an essential component of learning.

ESTABLISHING A RECORD

Portfolios, when employed to reach the highest potential for assessment, can allow for documentation of student growth in the processes of mulling over a topic; reading widely about the topic; discussing initial ideas with teachers, peers, and parents; reacting to feedback on drafts; and summarizing the substantive rethinking invested in revisions. Portfolios provide teachers and students with the opportunity to examine a record of the two most demanding learning processes: reflection and revision.

We can discuss the progress toward considering options, alternatives, and new insights if demanding exercises are placed before students and if they are given access to an information-rich environment. Teachers and students should be free to explore as many information outlets and formats as possible: The products eventually placed in the portfolio record reflect how both the teacher and learner contend with the information explosion. Products should show the evolution of the learner in reading, composition, revision, *and* the selection of documentation or literature that supports their writings.

When students do not learn the skills required for working with source materials in the early stages of reading and writing development, they find it difficult to cope with the shift to multiple sources. If they do not have the skills to work with multiple sources from a variety of formats, the typical term paper or composition assignment becomes an unfair task. The assignment is often undertaken with no sense of positive challenge because the student, and occasionally the teacher and school library media specialist, lack higher-level skills.

Many instructors emphasize library work. Locating sources, however, is largely a mechanical process, unlikely in itself to teach students to think or write about what they have read. If the research project (paper, debate, video, or oral presentation) is to be fully integrated into the composition requirements of any course, students must learn how to deal with sources of information. The emphasis should be on the analysis and synthesis of ideas and evidence beginning at the early stages of reading and writing. A portfolio allows for gathering products that reflect the evolution of the student's ability to critically select and use information.

The portfolio should include an ordered compilation of student products. These may be writings, recordings, drawings, diagrams, or any other means displaying student thought patterns. A casual gathering of papers one has written over a year or two probably does not deserve to be called a portfolio. A portfolio ideally should be a deliberate compilation, gathered according to a plan, for use by an identified reader or readers for specific needs or purposes.

A portfolio gathered for the teacher in a writing course may help with the teacher's instruction of a student. If submitted at the end of the course, the portfolio may help in the teacher's final student evaluation. A portfolio of writings gathered over a student's academic career may be examined by faculty for evidence of changes in the way the student thinks, reacts to problems, assesses data, and gives value to the information. Students may include their own reflections on their writings, as well as what has been read, viewed, observed, or heard. These reflections should give insight as to what the student thinks these pieces show about his or her strengths and weaknesses.

ALLOWING FOR COMPARISONS

Portfolios are most effective when students can compare earlier work in terms of progress in the level of sources used, selection of specific evidence and comparison of data, and growth in the depth of arguments presented. Written or recorded descriptive pieces (poetry, short stories, plays) can, over time, become more personal and more detailed. Readings, discussions, and viewings that have influenced this maturation process can be identified by the student author through the records placed in the portfolio.

The following list of abilities might serve as a beginning framework to identify some of the assessment areas toward which the teacher and library media specialist would strive in both their own teaching methods as well as in actual student performance. Students and educators should, through reading, writing, and conversation, demonstrate the ability to

- pose worthwhile questions;
- evaluate the adequacy of an argument;
- recognize facts, inferences, and opinions and use each appropriately;
- deal with quandaries and ill-formed problems that have no pat or unique solutions;
- give and receive criticism profitably;
- agree or disagree in degrees;

- extend a line of thought beyond the range of first impressions; and

- articulate a complex position without adding to its complexity.

These tasks are very demanding, and we would obviously see different levels of achievement based on experience, intelligence, guided practice, and extent of access to resources. To place some of these abilities within a more common framework, consider the following general progressive steps for the demonstration of elementary skills in reading and writing.

FOUNDATIONS IN READING
AND WRITING

A portfolio that documents the progress of an elementary student's *emergent reading* abilities would contain items that reflect the following stages:

1. Listens to story but is not looking at pages.

2. Watches pictures as adult reads story.

3. Makes up words for pictures.

4. Pretends to read.

5. Talks about each picture.

6. Participates in reading by supplying rhyming words.

7. Memorizes text and can pretend to read.

8. Recognizes words in a new context.

9. Reads word for word.

10. Reads familiar stories fluently.

11. Reads unfamiliar stories haltingly with little assistance.

12. Uses context clues, sentence structure, and phonic analysis to read new passages.

13. Voluntarily shares information with other children.

14. Seeks out and selects new sources of information.

15. Reads fluently from books and other materials.

Common stages that help to suggest documentation of an elementary school student's growth in *response to literature* (or other media) would probably be similar to the following:

1. Does not voluntarily respond to literature.

2. Asks you to read it again.

3. Tells whether likes the book.

4. Explains *why* likes or does not like a book.

5. Relates the book to own experiences or other books.

6. Analyzes something about the book: plot, setting, characters, illustrations.

7. Generalizes about the book with comments about the theme, type of book, author's purpose.

8. Develops criteria to evaluate the book.

The stages in elementary *writing development* are shown by the student's ability to move up the following levels:

1. Attempts to write in scribbles or draws patterns.

2. Pretends to write.

3. Writes mock letters.

4. Writes alphabet or mock letters around page.

5. Writes in a line across page.

6. Copies words seen around the room.

7. Writes alphabet letter strings.

8. Has message concept and tells what the message is.

9. Writes familiar words.

10. Writes a message.

11. Separates words with a space.

12. Writes lists.

13. Connects letters with sounds.

14. Labels drawings.

15. Summarizes a story in a single factual statement.

16. Invents spelling.

17. Writes several short sentences.

18. Uses both phonics and sight to spell words.

19. Writes the start of a story.

20. Begins to use punctuation.

21. Uses revisions to add to the story.

22. Writes for several different purposes: narrative, expository, persuasive.

23. Writes a short story with beginning, middle, end.

24. Willingly revises.

25. Spells more conventionally.

26. Retells familiar story; follows pattern of known story.

27. Uses details, dialogue, expresses emotion.

28. Uses commas, quotation marks, apostrophes.

29. Writes clearly; message makes sense to wider audience.

30. Writes original poetry.

31. Writes creatively and imaginatively.

32. Willingly revises and edits.

33. Uses writing techniques to create suspense or humor.

34. Employs a wide variety of strategies for revision and editing.

Several of these abilities are more easily documented than others, but the challenge is to create learning situations in which students can demonstrate their abilities, practice, and provide evidence of progress. Use of video and audio recorders may be the only means of documenting some of the stages, but written products will be the most common.

A PORTFOLIO OF
INFORMATION SKILLS

Carol Kuhlthau offered an extensive grade-by-grade activities list in 1981 that could serve as a beginning point for determining the specific library use skills or abilities to be documented. Her checklists include both location and interpretation skill levels through the early secondary school years. From such an extensive list, as well as from many others available in the literature and through state curricular guides, we have yet to determine the key items that should be included in a portfolio of student information skills performance. Recent library skill guides are giving greater attention to student use of on-line and multimedia information systems. With each advancement in technology, a new set of abilities or skills seems to result.

This growing list of search skills can be a part of the portfolio content, especially if it allows library media specialists the opportunity to show teachers, parents, and principals examples of student mastery of computerized information technologies. The basic questions related to information use, application, or interpretation probably do *not* change over time. Kuhlthau's more recent works that attempt to define the "library research process" for the average student take us closer to the experiences that can be best documented and traced through a portfolio.

Within the framework of the following questions, evidence of progressive writing experiences and information search experiences should be gathered by the library media specialist in order to document student performance. Michael Marland published this list of questions for the information curriculum in 1981. Additional comments follow each question in order to provide suggestions as to skills that might be documented in information literacy portfolios.

1. *What do I need to do?* Ability to analyze the information task; analyze the audience's information need or demand; describe a plan of operation; select important and useful questions and narrow or define focus of assignment; describe possible issues to be investigated.

2. *Where could I go?* Ability to determine best initial leads for relevant information; determine possible immediate access to background information

(gaining the "larger picture"); consider information sources within and beyond the library.

3. *How do I get to the information?* Ability to determine best modes of wider information access; what is possible and reasonable within the time limitations and expectations of the assignment or information need; identify options and alternatives including various information formats and delivery systems.

4. *Which resources shall I use?* Ability to identify relevant materials; sense relationships between information items; determine which resources are most likely to be authoritative and reliable; consider and state the advantages and disadvantages of bias present in resources; consider discovered facts and search for counterfacts; consider stated and personal opinions and search for counteropinions; determine extent of need for historical perspective.

5. *How shall I use the resources?* Determine if information is pertinent to the topic; estimate the adequacy of the information; test validity of the information; focus on specific issues within the boundaries of information obtained; group data in categories according to appropriate criteria; determine the advantages and disadvantages of different information formats and intellectual levels.

6. *Of what should I make a record?* Extract significant ideas and summarize supporting, illustrative details; define a systematic method to gather, sort, and retrieve data; combine critical concepts into a statement of conclusions; restate major ideas of a complex topic in concise form; separate a topic into major components according to appropriate criteria; sequence information and data in order to emphasize specific arguments or issues.

7. *Have I got the information I need?* Recognize instances in which more than one interpretation of material is valid and necessary; demonstrate that the information obtained is relevant to the issues of importance; if necessary, state a hypothesis or theme and match evidence to the focused goal of the paper or project; reflect, edit, revise, and determine if previous information search and analysis steps should be repeated.

8. *How should I present it?* Place data in tabular form using charts, graphs, or illustrations; match illustrations and verbal descriptions for best impact; note relationships between or among data, opinions, or other forms of information; propose a new plan, create a new system, interpret historical events, and predict likely future happenings; analyze the background and potential for reception of ideas and arguments of the intended audience; communicate orally and in writing to teachers and among peers.

9. *What have I achieved?* Accept and give constructive criticism; reflect and revise again; describe most valuable sources of information; estimate the adequacy of the information acquired and the need for additional resources;

state future questions or themes for investigation; seek feedback from a variety of audiences.

This is a very challenging menu of possible areas for measurement of student ability and action. We don't know which of these areas are best documented through a portfolio, nor have we experienced the conversations that will probably bring many additional abilities to our attention. The list given for student abilities in information literacy provides a beginning framework for establishing assignments that will result in student products for the portfolio.

STUDENT REFLECTION

Finally, and most important, students will need to reflect through written statements and interviews following completion of the product in order to express those information literacy abilities they feel they have practiced and at what level they feel they are operating. Teachers and library media specialists will add their insights to the level of the student's performance.

In order for educators to establish meaningful information literacy exercises that challenge the student, assessment is best undertaken by means of a progressive portfolio of the student's work. Both the teacher and the library media specialist must think in terms of assignments that establish a broad range of sources the student will need to investigate and that are developed in recognition of the equally broad range of responses the student might produce.

Of major importance are the techniques of modeling information literacy skills developed by the teacher and the library media specialist and the establishment of inquiry environments in which students work together in order to explore and share the challenges of information search and selection. The potential for development of student information literacy portfolios may not be fully reached until educators move more deeply into electronic record-keeping practices. The time is ripe to go beyond the simple tests of the past in our explorations of what can be observed, what can be discussed, and what abilities can be enhanced.

INFORMATION LITERACY AND PORTFOLIO RESOURCES

Ballard, Leslie. "Portfolios and Self-Assessment." *English Journal* 81 (1992): 46-48.

Beach, Richard, and Lillian S. Bridwell. *New Directions in Composition Research.* New York: Guilford, 1984.

Belanoff, Pat, and Marcia Dickson, eds. *Portfolios: Process and Product.* Portsmouth, NH: Boynton/Cook, 1991.

Browne, M. Neil, and Stuart M. Keeley. *Asking the Right Questions.* Englewood Cliffs, NJ: Prentice-Hall, 1990.

Bunda, Mary Anne. "Capturing the Richness of Student Outcomes with Qualitative Techniques." *New Directions for Institutional Research* 72 (1991): 35-47.

Cooper, Winfield, and B. J. Brown. "Using Portfolios to Empower Student Writers." *English Journal* 81 (1992): 40-45.

Farr, Roger. "Setting Directions for Language Arts Portfolios." *Educational Leadership* 48 (1990): 103.

———. *Portfolios: Assessment in Language Arts*. ERIC Document Reproduction Service No. ED 334 603, 1991.

Frederick, Betz, and Cathy Stafford. "Getting Ready for ASAP: The Making of a Portfolio." *Arizona Reading Journal* 20 (1991): 36-40.

Gillespie, Cindy. "Questions About Student-Generated Questions." *Journal of Reading* 34 (1990): 250-57.

Graves, Donald H., and Bonnie S. Sunstein, eds. *Portfolio Portraits*. Portsmouth, NH: Heinemann, 1992.

Hamm, Mary, and Dennis Adams. "Portfolio: It's Not Just for Artists Anymore." *Science Teacher* 58 (1991): 18-21.

Irving, A., and W. Snape. *Educating Library Users in Secondary Schools*. British Library Research and Development Report 5467, 1979.

Krest, Margie. "Adapting the Portfolio to Meet Student Needs." *English Journal* 79 (1990): 29-34.

Kuhlthau, Carol Collier. *School Librarian's Grade-by-Grade Activities Program*. West Nyack, NY: Center for Applied Research in Education, 1981.

———. *Teaching the Library Research Process*. West Nyack, NY: Center for Applied Research in Education, 1985.

———. *Information Skills for an Information Society: A Review of Research*. Syracuse, NY: ERIC Clearinghouse on Information Resources, 1987.

Lamme, Linda Leonard, and Cecilia Hysmith. "One School's Adventure into Portfolio Assessment." *Language Arts* 68 (1991): 629-40.

Lane, Barry. *After "The End": Teaching and Learning Creative Revision*. Portsmouth, NH: Heinemann, 1992.

Maeroff, Gene I. "Assessing Alternative Assessment." *Phi Delta Kappan* 73 (1991): 273-81.

Marland, Michael. *Information Skills in the Secondary Curriculum*. London: Methuen Educational, 1981.

Moffett, James. *Detecting Growth in Language*. Portsmouth, NH: Boynton/Cook, 1992.

Moss, Pamela A., Jamie Sue Beck, and Roberta Heter. "Portfolios: Accountability, and an Interactive Approach to Validity." *Educational Measurement: Issues and Practice* 11 (1992): 12-21.

Murphy, Sandra, and Mary Ann Smith. "Talking About Portfolios." *Quarterly of the National Writing Project and the Center for the Study of Writing* 12 (1990): 1-27.

National Council for the Social Studies Task Force on Scope and Sequence. "In Search of a Scope and Sequence for Social Studies." *Social Education* 53 (1989): 376-87.

Newkirk, Thomas, and Nancie Atwell, eds. *Understanding Writing: Ways of Observing, Learning, and Teaching.* Portsmouth, NH: Heinemann, 1988.

Nweke, Winifred. *What Type of Evidence Is Provided Through Portfolio Assessment Method?* ERIC Document Reproduction Service No. ED 340 719, 1991.

Paulson, F., P. Paulson, and C. Meyer. "What Makes a Portfolio a Portfolio?" *Educational Leadership* 48 (1991): 60-63.

Rhodes, Lynn K. *Literacy Assessment: A Handbook of Instruments.* Portsmouth, NH: Heinemann, 1992.

Rousculp, Edwin E., and Gerald H. Maring. "Portfolios for a Community of Learners." *Journal of Reading* 35 (1992): 378-85.

Spatt, Brenda. *Writing from Sources.* New York: St. Martin's Press, 1991.

Valencia, Sheila W. "A Portfolio Approach to Classroom Assessment." *Reading Teacher* 43 (1990): 338-40.

Valencia, Sheila W., and Scott G. Paris. "Portfolio Assessment for Young Readers." *Reading Teacher* 44 (1991): 680-82.

Valeri-Gold, Maria, James R. Olson, and Mary P. Deming. "Portfolios: Collaborative Authentic Assessment Opportunities for College Development Learners." *Journal of Reading* 35 (1992): 298-305.

Vavrus, Linda. "Put Portfolios to the Test." *Instructor* 100 (1990): 48-53.

Wells, Gordon, and Gen Ling Chang-Wells. *Constructing Knowledge Together: Classrooms as Centers of Inquiry and Literacy.* Portsmouth, NH: Heinemann, 1992.

Wiggins, Grant. "A True Test: Toward More Authentic and Equitable Assessment." *Phi Delta Kappan* 70 (1989): 703-13.

11

Assessing the Big Outcomes

 Nora Redding

What does a good problem solver look like? How does an expert decision maker differ from a novice? What evidence convinces parents that their child is a self-directed or a collaborative worker?

These are questions educators everywhere are facing as we take on the responsibility of preparing students for a future that promises to be far different from the present. In the old days, our job of validating students' recall of information was easy. Today, judging their abilities to perform complex tasks requires a totally different type of assessment.

Aurora Public Schools in Colorado has been struggling with this assessment problem since we began implementing five new district outcomes. A result of strategic planning the Five Outcomes are nontraditional, future-oriented abilities students will need to be productive citizens of the 21st century. Our district has taken on the mission of graduating students who are

1. self-directed learners,

2. collaborative workers,

3. complex thinkers,

4. quality producers, and

5. community contributors.

Our intent is not that these Five Outcomes be framed, hung on every wall, and subsequently ignored, but that they become our curriculum, the focus of our instruction, and eventually our graduation requirements. But to know when students have achieved the Five Outcomes and to be able to document that achievement required a radical change in assessment.

PROBLEMS ENCOUNTERED

Although we had an abundance of energy and talent, the job was not as simple as we had hoped. Thinking up assessment tasks was easy, but specifying the criteria and quality standards by which student performance would be judged was beyond our expertise.

We ran into three problems. First, although teachers were clear about the subject-area concepts, principles, and skills they wanted to see demonstrated, they were unsure about the critical characteristics of such things as effective problem solving or working collaboratively or making a contribution to the community.

Second, there was little continuity in criteria from one task to another. For example, the list of self-directed behaviors the business teachers wanted students to demonstrate differed widely from the qualities the social studies teachers identified. How could we communicate to students what they must do to demonstrate proficiency if we couldn't agree among ourselves?

And last, because our criteria were based on subjective judgments, there was no way to maintain interrater reliability or ensure the integrity of our standards. How good was good enough?

GETTING HELP

Fortunately we knew where to go for help. Just "down the street" from us is the Mid-Continent Regional Educational Laboratory (McREL). Through his work during the past three years developing Dimensions of Learning, a comprehensive learning model, Bob Marzano and others at McREL had developed an assessment framework that provided the model we needed. The critical part of the model was McREL's identification of 14 complex thinking processes, such as problem solving, decision making, invention, experimental inquiry, and others. Each complex thinking process was described step-by-step or with the critical components listed. Accompanying each step or component was a detailed four-step scoring guide, or *rubric*, that described what varying degrees of mastery or quality looked like for each step or component. Two things were apparent. First, the 14 complex thinking processes "fleshed out" our third outcome, Complex Thinkers, and could be immediately assimilated into our mode. Second, we could define our remaining four outcomes in terms of components and accompanying scoring guides in the McREL Assessment Framework.

Using the McREL personnel as our consultants, we first developed 19 characteristics from our Five Outcomes (see fig. 11.1). For each characteristic we developed a four-step rubric to describe an exceptional performer (level 4), a competent performed (level 3—our target), and two stages of novice performers (levels 2 and 1).

For example, an expert (level 4) performer on characteristic Number 1 (sets priorities and achievable goals) meets the following criteria: "Consistently develops clear expectations and challenging goals; perceives the value of goals and their accomplishment; has a clear sense of own physical, mental, and emotional abilities, and strives to work close to the edge of competence; shows maturity of judgment in the establishment of priorities; knows the criteria for success before beginning work." A level 1 performer, on the other hand, "seldom develops clear expectations,

A Self-Directed Learner

1. Sets priorities and achievable goals.
2. Monitors and evaluates progress.
3. Creates options for self.
4. Assumes responsibility for actions.
5. Creates a positive vision for self and future.

A Collaborative Worker

6. Monitors own behavior as a group member.
7. Assesses and manages group functioning.
8. Demonstrates interactive communication.
9. Demonstrates consideration for individual differences.

A Complex Thinker

10. Uses a wide variety of strategies for managing complex issues.
11. Selects strategies appropriate to the resolution of complex issues and applies the strategies with accuracy and thoroughness.
12. Accesses and uses topic-relevant knowledge.

A Quality Producer

13. Creates products that achieve their purpose.
14. Creates products appropriate to the intended audience.
15. Creates products that reflect craftsmanship.
16. Uses appropriate resources/technology.

A Community Contributor

17. Demonstrates knowledge about his or her diverse communities.
18. Takes action.
19. Reflects on role as a community contributor.

Fig. 11.1. Aurora Public Schools' Five Outcomes.

goals; rarely considers physical, mental, emotional limitations or abilities; has difficulty finding value in the task; rarely considers priorities or criteria."

The descriptors for judging student achievement are the same for all grade levels. While a 1st grader might set goals about what stories he or she could read in a day and a high school senior about writing a term paper, the assessment criteria for judging goals-setting ability remain the same K-12.

TWO EXAMPLES

Using our 19 district-developed rubrics and the McREL rubrics for the 14 complex thinking processes, teachers and curriculum developers have been designing assessment tasks that fuse subject area content with the Five Outcomes. The difference between traditional assessment and our new performance-based assessments can be illustrated by comparing the final exam for a Photography 2 class with a revised assessment developed by two art teachers, Dana Breese and Randee Perkins.

Dana and Randee analyzed the existing Photo 2 final (take and develop 10 high quality photographs) to see which of our five outcomes were being addressed. They concluded that students' grades were based on two of the Quality Producer characteristics: creating products that reflect craftsmanship (Number 15), and using appropriate resources and technology (Number 16). The two teachers decided to revise the assessment to include complex thinking and community contributing. (Keep in mind that we consider the school and the people in the school as part of the community.) Figure 11.2 shows the resulting final assessment.

---

1. You are representing an ad agency. Your job is to find a client in the school who needs photos to promote his/her program. (Examples: the Teen Mothers' program, the fine arts program, Student Congress.)

2. Your job is to research all the possibilities, select a program, learn about that program, and then record on film the excitement and unique characteristics that make up the program you have selected. Your photos will be used to advertise and stimulate interest in that area.

3. Previsualize how you will illustrate your ideas by either writing descriptions or by drawing six of your proposed frames. Present these six ideas to your instructor (the director of the ad agency) before you shoot.

Fig. 11.2. Photo 2 Exam—Promotional Advertisement.

The complex thinking task Dana and Randee chose from the McREL list of complex thinking processes was *invention*. By changing their original assessment task (apply photo knowledge and skills to produce 10 photographs) to an invention, they made the task more challenging and relevant to the real world, and they began collecting data on students' ability to reach three of our five outcomes instead of just one.

As assessment criteria, they chose four from the *invention* rubric, changing the generic wording to make it specific to this task. For example, they selected the question "Was the situation identified by the student as needing improvement important or noteworthy?" and rewrote it as "Did the student select a program with a viable need?" They also wrote a fifth criterion to cover the student's use of photography knowledge and skills. Having identified the five criteria for assessing student performance, the two teachers assigned weights to each criterion and constructed an assessment sheet to show students how much each trait would be emphasized. Again using the *invention* rubric as a model, the teachers produced their own four-step rubric to describe exceptional, competent, and novice performance in each of their five criteria. For the first criterion, "Did the student select a program with a viable need?" the rubric reads:

> *Level 4*: The student selects a program needing promotion. That need has not been recognized before, or the promotion could result in an improvement others have missed. Filling the need of the program will have important consequences.

> *Level 3*: The student selects a program that could be improved upon through promotion. Meeting that need will have important consequences.

> *Level 2*: The student selects a program that could benefit from further promotion. Meeting that need might be only moderately important.

> *Level 1*: The student selects a program with a need that is not important or is of very minor importance.

Students know that level 3 is the standard that all work must reach and level 4 is exemplary work.

While some teachers developed an assessment by revising an existing test, other teachers started from scratch. A U.S. history assessment written by social studies teacher Ray E. Jenkins illustrates the general planning process.

As the focus of a unit on the civil rights movement, Ray *identified key facts, concepts, and principles* he wanted all students to remember. Among those were the principles that (1) key leaders have a profound effect on the course of history, and (2) history looks different from different personal or group perspectives.

Next, Ray *selected one of the thinking processes* from the McREL list to structure an assessment task around. He chose decision making and developed the following simulation for students. "It is June 15, 1968. You represent one of the civil rights organizations (NAACP, Urban League, Black Panthers). Martin Luther King, Jr., has recently been assassinated. What direction should the movement take?"

Ray knew that the decision-making task addressed District Outcome Number 3, Complex Thinking. He then decided to *build other district outcomes into the task*. He chose to structure the task with students working in small groups and assess students on their collaborative skills—Outcome Number 2. He also decided to have students role-play the leader of the organization in a final discussion (or argument) and assess the quality of that performance—Outcome Number 4.

Finally, from the 19 district characteristics and from the McREL decision-making criteria, Ray chose those traits on which students would be assessed. Adjusting the generic wording to make it specific to the task, Ray wrote the following five criteria.

- Did your group's decision and your participation in the role-playing reveal an accurate understanding of the essential facts, concepts, and principles of the civil rights movement?

- Did your group select appropriate and important alternatives to be considered?

- Did your group's final decision meet the decision criteria for the organization your represented, and was it true to the beliefs of that organization?

- As your group worked to collect information and come to a decision, did you personally assess and manage group functioning?

- As you participated in the role-playing discussion, did you achieve the purpose of being true to the organization you represented?

WHAT IS GAINED?

The changes in assessment procedures in Aurora Public Schools have produced significant benefits for both students and teachers.

Alignment with district goals. Classroom instruction and assessment are being precisely aligned with district goals. While teaching important information about photography or U.S. history, teachers also extend students' skills in such areas as inventing, decision making, and working collaboratively. At the same time, teachers collect reliable information about their individual students' abilities to reach the five district outcomes.

Improved instruction. Students are engaged in their own learning because the tasks they are given are meaningful and intriguing. Knowing the assessment criteria up front, they take responsibility for becoming prepared and use their teacher as resource and coach.

Improved learning. More active student involvement in interesting tasks results in improved learning. For example, the students and teachers who filled Ray's doorway on the day of the civil rights role-playing can attest to the high level of knowledge students exhibited about the civil rights movement. Students themselves reported on the powerful insights they had gained.

KNOWING WHAT IS EXPECTED

The assessment model is a good one. Having a framework of criteria and descriptive rubrics, all developed from stated district outcomes, provides focus for educators and students. Teachers have flexibility of choice within the framework but consistency of standards. Students know what is expected.

Learning to apply the model will take time. As more and more teachers are introduced to it, the model will surely be changed, but we feel we have taken solid steps toward solving the problem of assessing the "big" outcomes. The results will be improved planning, improved instruction, and improved student achievement, with graduates who are equipped to meet the complex problems of the 21st century.

12

Linking Assessment to Accountability: Sixth-Grade Performance Assessment

 Willa Spicer and Joyce Sherman

WHAT IS IT?

It is 10 A.M. on Friday morning. Marcia and two of her friends are walking nervously toward the faculty room where two assessors the girls have never met are awaiting them with a small audience of younger children from their school. Marcia knows she should not be nervous; she has made two full presentations to selected audiences during the year. And after all, one of those audiences included her mother and father. She has done her research, using her time carefully and using the criteria sheet to check off her own progress.

Still she worries. The two other girls carry oak tag posters, one a collage of civil rights activities and one a large Venn diagram comparing the North and South in 1860. Marcia carries a a different type of visual to go with her speech, and she wonders now whether she has taken too much of a risk.

"Welcome," says the nice looking woman as the girls enter. "I am Mrs. Jones and I teach in Pennsylvania. With me is Mr. Vonn who works for Johnson and Johnson. We are both looking forward to your presentation. Please sit over there so that you can see the other presentations." Marcia and her friends find seats with the three boys who are already in the room. They quickly exchange good luck signs.

Mrs. Jones talks briefly with the group of fourth- and fifth-graders who will be the audience for the presentation and then turns to the presenters. "Marcia," she says, "let's begin with you."

"I hope I don't let you down," Marcia's friend whispers as Marcia gathers her note cards.

"Just do it like we practiced."

Marcia stands square before her audience. "My question," she announces, "is 'What is comedy?' " She pauses. Her friend walks forward and throws a pie in her face. The audience bursts into laughter. Marcia wipes her face, picks up her notecards, and takes a deep breath. "There are three types of comedy," she begins.

The purpose of South Brunswick (NJ) School System's Sixth-Grade Perform-ance Assessment is to measure the ability of our students to research and present information. The assessment provides students with performance experience and helps them learn how to improve their performance abilities. We want to teach students the standards of high performance and then show them how to reach that standard.

During the two to three weeks preceding the scheduled start of the performance assessment, all sixth-grade students are asked to write two social studies-based researchable questions related to the "American experience." The teacher and librarian meet to review these questions and select one that is workable within the confines of the resources in the school. On the date the assessment begins, one question is returned to the student and he or she has eight hours to complete the following tasks:

- Research the question using a variety of sources

- Prepare a bibliography

- Prepare a written report

- Prepare a three to five minute oral presentation

- Prepare a visual presentation to accompany oral report.

No notes or materials can be brought from home nor can any of the research be taken home during the process. Students have access to all the school resources that the building team believes is important to their success. No help can be given by the teacher. In most cases, all of the work is done in the library with the teacher not present. The librarian is available to act as coach. She answers questions for students and reminds them where things can be found. She may not, however, tell any student what to do. Students completely control the management of their time. The way in which the eight hours are scheduled is determined by each school, but a familiar model is four hours per day (9:15-12:15 and 1:30-2:30, for example) for two consecutive days (see fig. 12.1).

Following the eight hours of preparation, students are scheduled for an oral presentation before a panel of trained judges and a small audience of students (usually fifth-graders, giving them an opportunity to become familiar with what will be expected of them the following year). The judges are also given the students' written work and the students' efforts are assessed in the categories of research strategies, written report, oral presentation, and visual presentation (see figs. 12.2, 12.3, and 12.4). There are two assessors for every 8-9 students. A five-point rating scale is used for each category. Overall scores of 17-20 are considered excellent, 13-16 very good, 12-13 good, 5-11 limited, and 1-4 poor. When the assessment is complete, students write a personal narrative in two parts: (1) a reflection of their own experience and (2) a reflection on this type of assessment. Both parts of the narrative may include suggestions for changes. All students work within these parameters. Classified students may receive help from the Resource Room teacher if they request it, but in all other respects they follow the same set of rules.

HISTORY

The South Brunswick School System had been involved in portfolio assessment for young children for several years before issues related to assessment of older children were raised. Two issues led to consideration of new methods of assessment.

(*Text continues on page 141.*)

Teacher	Groups of Std.	Research Days	Research Times	Presentation Day	Presentation Time	Presentation Space	Assessor Time	Assessor space	Audience
Kowalski	Group 1-6 Std. Group 2-7 Std.	Mon. May 24 Tues. May 25	9:30-12:00 1:30-3:00	Wed. May 26	10:30-11:30	Gp 1-Lillian Gp 2-Faculty	11:30-12:30 (approx.)	Gp 1-Purple Rm Gp 2-Turner Rm	Kowalski's 5 Gp 1-6 Gp 2-5
Warms	Group 1-6 Std. Group 2-6 Std. Group 3-5 Std. Group 4-5 Std.	Wed. May 26 Thurs. May 27	9:30-12:00 1:30-3:00	Fri. May 28	10:30-11:30	Gp 1-Music Gp 2-Small Gym Gp 3-Faculty Gp 4-Lillian	11:30-12:30 (approx.)	Library	Pollard Gp 1-6 Gp 2-6 Gp 3-6 Gp 4-7
Jamet	Group 1-7 Std. Group 2-7 Std. Group 3-7 Std.	Tues. June 1 Wed. June 2	9:30-12:00 1:30-3:00	Thurs. June 3	10:30-11:30	Gp 1-Faculty Gp 2-Lillian Gp 3-Small Gym	11:30-12:30 (approx.)	Library	Spangenberg Gp 1-8 Std. Gp 2-8 Std. Gp 3-9 Std.

Fig. 12.1. Sixth-Grade Assessment Schedule.

Criteria for Performance Assessment—South Brunswick Schools

Name of Student _____   Name of School _____

Question: _____

Written Scale

Please indicate the number which best describes the overall quality of the written work.
If the student can do everything at one point but not at the next, mark .5 (for example,
there could be a score of 3.5).

5. *Complete, well written, elaborate, convincing*
   The student clearly responds to the question and elaborates on the question as well as
      its importance.
   Details and examples are given to fully support the answer in question.
   An introductory paragraph clearly shapes the question and the concluding paragraph
      has clarity and insight.
   The writing is engaging, organized, and fluid.
   Sentence structure is varied and mechanics are correct. (No obtrusive errors)
   Varied sources are organized alphabetically, including author (if known), title, and
      publication information.

4. *Complete, convincing, conclusive, competently written*
   The student addresses question through introductory paragraph.
   The student sufficiently answers question and provides some supporting details.
   The writing is interesting and organized.
   Structure and mechanics are consistently correct.
   Concluding paragraph is included and varied sources are cited in an organized way.

3. *Basically competent: satisfied requirements*
   The student states the question.
   He/she answers the question with a small amount of supporting information.
   There is a basic organization but it is not always clear.
   The structure and mechanics are generally correct with some errors.

2. *Inconclusive or unclear*
   The student has a question but the answers and/or conclusions are undeveloped or irrelevant.
   Basic information may be lacking.
   The writing may lack organization and be difficult to follow.
   There may be many errors of sentence structure and mechanics.
   Sources may be mentioned.

1. *Incomplete, incoherent, poorly written*
   The student does not state the question.
   No answer or conclusion is given.
   Writing is disorganized and difficult to read.
   Sentence structure and mechanics are consistently weak.
   Sources may or may not be noted.

TOTAL WRITTEN SCORE _____

Assessor's Comments:

Fig. 12.2. Criteria for Performance Assessment, Written Scale.

Criteria for Performance Assessment—South Brunswick Schools

Name of Student _____   Name of School _____

Question: _____

Trait Scales

Circle the number that best reflects the presentation. Add the numbers and provide a total score.

1_____1/2_____0

| The presentation totally fulfills all elements of the criteria as stated. | The presentation only partially fulfills the criteria as stated. | The presentation does not fulfill the criteria as stated. |

Visual

The visual presentation:

is neat and easily visible	1	1/2	0
shows student creativity	1	1/2	0
appropriate and engaging to its audience	1	1/2	0
clearly enhances the question studied	1	1/2	0
is a well-integrated part of the overall presentation	1	1/2	0

TOTAL VISUAL _____

Oral

In the oral presentation, the student:

has a clear and interesting introduction to the topic	1	1/2	0
speaks clearly, audibly, and with inflection	1	1/2	0
uses eye contact	1	1/2	0
uses verbal strategies that engage the audience (such as metaphors, rhetorical questions, colorful examples, strong verbs)	1	1/2	0
gives relevant supporting data to convincingly answer the question	1	1/2	0

TOTAL ORAL _____

Fig. 12.3. Criteria for Performance Assessment, Trait Scales.

First, a new school and the redistricting of the elementary student population raised questions about the degree to which programs in the various schools were equitable to the children in the whole community. Did all of the children have equal opportunities to learn? Did staff at every school have equally high expectations for children? Second, a change in the cultural understanding about assessment began to emerge from the experience early childhood teachers were having with literacy portfolios. Teachers began to realize that assessment could enhance instruction and contribute

Criteria for Performance Assessment—South Brunswick Schools

Name of Student _____   Name of School _____

Question: _____

Process Scale

The student shows evidence of a plan designed to achieve written, oral,
    and visual goals.   1   1/2   0

The student's plan is appropriate to accomplish the task.   1   1/2   0

The student demonstrates that he/she can use available resources to locate
    appropriate materials.   1   1/2   0

The student shows evidence of using writing process: note taking, drafting,
    revising, editing.   1   1/2   0

The student can critique, reflect on, or analyze the progress of his/her work. 1   1/2   0

TOTAL PROCESS _____

TOTAL SCORE _____

Names of Assessors:

Fig. 12.4. Criteria for Performance Assessment, Process Scale.

to learning, and that assessment was something teachers did rather than something
done to them.

By the time it was proposed that the South Brunswick School System develop
a set of outcome statements for the elementary schools, teachers had learned that
complex intellectual purposes could be measured. Thus, the list of outcomes supports high-level performance. The teachers putting the list together did not censor
out items that could not be measured. Rather, they believed they were to cite the
most important outcomes of elementary education and that all the items could and
would be measured in some way or another (see fig. 12.5).

It would be hard to overestimate the importance of the teachers' mindset to
implementing change. The social studies curriculum had a required research component in it for every grade, and when that curriculum was revised in 1983, the
research component was reaffirmed by all audiences. Still, librarians regularly
reported that what passed as research was simply answering a factual question or
researching a topic such as whales or Michigan. Research consisted of looking up
the topic in the encyclopedia, or as the common wisdom decreed, using three
different sources whether they were needed or not. No manner of in-service training
or inspirational speakers could change the lip-service about good research into
consistent classroom practice.

When students leave grade 6, they should:

Use information and concepts studied in social studies and science during the elementary years •#

Recall core information set forth in the various curricula

Identify, express, and solve problems (math, verbal and visual) •+

Enjoy reading, writing, and problem solving

Take risks and experiment with language, numbers, and visuals *•

Ask a question that is appropriate for research *

Identify the type of information needed for a task, locate that information, and organize it appropriately *•

Present information and ideas clearly through written, visual, and oral means, demonstrating awareness of audience *#•+

Present ideas through one or more of the following: art, music, dance, writing, construction #

Make choices among the methods of expression and know which are most appropriate for them and for the task #+

Explain the processes and procedures (strategies) they use and explain why they were chosen #•+

Work successfully alone *•

Work successfully as part of a group #+

Persevere at a difficult or complex task *#•+

Take ownership of their work and take pride in it *#+

Show initiative *#•+

---

* Research Assessment, February. 1991
# Arts Assessment, June 1991
• Math Assessment, June 1991
+ Problem-Solving Assessment

Fig. 12.5. Holistic Statements About Important Things Sixth-Graders Should Be Able to Do When They Leave the Elementary Schools.

Most of the librarians and some of the teachers realized that something beyond the ordinary was needed. They were serious about teaching students to locate, organize, and present information effectively. Thus, the impetus to change was already in place when members of the South Brunswick staff met the people from the Mark Twain School in Littleton, Colorado, who, under the direction of Grant Wiggins, were already engaged in performance assessment of fifth-graders. There were champions for change in the system, and there was a growing tradition of authentic assessment at the school level. The Littleton experience, therefore, was relevant for our purposes and met important systemic needs.

The outline of the task and the components of the scales are the same today as those used by The Mark Twain School to measure the effectiveness of their instruction. After several years of experience, however, only the outlines remain. South Brunswick has adapted the Littleton work for its own purpose, and at least three school districts have adapted our work similarly.

The process of making the assessment our own had two major components. First all fifth- and sixth-grade teachers and librarians considered what to measure and how to measure it. Second, each aspect of the assessment would be reviewed and revised every year. We field tested the performance assessment in selected classes at three elementary schools.

Now there was a risk. There was no training of the children first—no coaching or teacher training. Just a group of teachers and librarians willing to say that, if we wanted students to have some level of proficiency in research, we should find out if they have it. The principals also took a risk that first year. Permitting students to work completely on their own for eight hours seemed foolhardy to many. But the principals also agreed that if we wanted students to persevere and to engage in complex intellectual tasks, we ought to find out if they could work independently.

To no one's real surprise, the students were anything but proficient. Many failed to edit their work; the majority did not cite their sources; 90% used a piece of oak tag with a picture for their visual, and as many read their written report and called it their oral presentation. They did, however, persevere and they were engaged for the entire time. Despite the fact that their products were, on the whole, mediocre, they understood the process.

We were pleased. We had our first data about student performance. We could stop cursing the darkness. Now we only had to teach students how to use their time more profitably, how to use criteria to measure good work, how to write and answer questions, how to give an oral report, and how to use a visual to enhance presentation.

Staff members began to coach students on research. Almost every sixth-grade class began to practice, and many fourth- and fifth-grade teachers began to use parts of the scales to help students assess their own work. Assignments changed in grades 4-6 as teachers began to understand the nature of the assessment.

Meanwhile, fifth- and sixth-grade teachers and librarians reviewed both the task and the scales. We were helped by researchers from ETS (Educational Testing Service) who joined our deliberations.

As the teachers worked with the students and began to use the scales, both the form and the content of the scales changed. ETS researchers taught us to think about whether the task was holistic. That is, no measure of the components of the task could stand alone. After deliberation, we kept the writing task holistic (see figs. 12.2, 12.3, and 12.4). In the case of the oral report and the visual and process scales, we decided that the component parts were important separately and built a trait scale for each area. Thus, if a student can speak clearly or make eye contact during his or her oral report, that skill is noted and reported.

We also reviewed the logistics. The field test was fairly easy. Perhaps 100 students were involved. Now we were going to move to more than 300 students, each having two assessors.

The assessors had to be trained. The decision to take assessors from outside the district seemed politically important as well as expedient. Many people wanted to learn about performance and we invited them all in to participate. Thus, last year we had over 125 assessors representing local business; district parents and teachers; administrators and teachers from districts as far away as Virginia and Toronto, Canada; and students from local colleges. In addition, we hosted a full class of students from a Pennsylvania college for a full week. They worked with students and teachers in the classrooms and studied our processes and participated in extensive training before they were assessors.

The training of assessors has improved over time. We now have benchmark papers for each level on the writing scale and we train both children and adults using these papers. We have yet to develop good benchmarks for the oral or visual sections but are working on that. We collect the data from the assessors carefully, asking each person to record his or her score separately. ETS is evaluating the data from the researchers, trying to guage reliability. Of the many issues related to using outside assessors, one of the more interesting is whether or not different categories of assessors score differently from each other.

Finally, we have found more and more ways to use the data. We find that students who read and write competently may not have the highest scores on standardized tests. Given the chance to work without adult direction, we find that the major intelligences of children are reflected in the way they work—artists answer their questions first in visuals, mathematicians make charts, and verbal learners begin by writing. We find that the community and Board of Education understand our program better because we take them data and scales.

We continue to review and revise all aspects of this assessment. The teachers and librarians meet; they argue about what research is; they consider alternatives, and they examine ways to make children more competent researchers. It is in the reflection that assessment works. Learning becomes visible to students, staff members, and parents.

IMPACT ON THE SCHOOL LIBRARY PROGRAM

From the time South Brunswick School System attended the New Jersey State Library's Cape May Conference in the fall of 1987, we have been intellectually committed to the concept of resource-based teaching as introduced to us by Dr. David Loertscher at that conference. However, to build this intellectual commitment into practical reality has proven challenging. There are a number of reasons for this. Change is always difficult, and time constraints mean that collaborative effort must be perceived as having a significant "payoff" for it to be embraced enthusiastically. In spite of a good deal of effort, the resource-based teaching model did not interest many teachers at first and was being implemented only sporadically. However, as the performance assessment has become a reality, as teachers at all levels have perceived it as a measurement of significant goals and outcomes, and as instruction has begun to be driven by the assessment, we are now experiencing a significant shift in the development of true collegial relationships between the librarian and teachers. The teachers are *requesting* collaborative partnerships to develop and carry out units of study.

We have outlined the research, writing, and library skill goals we want to emphasize at each grade level (see fig. 12.6). This is a management device to assure inclusion of these objectives in the curriculum and in no way limits us, for example, from using all writing models at each level. Now, after teachers identify their social studies units for the year, they meet individually with the librarian to plan one unit of study which will be constructed and delivered collaboratively with the librarian and will incorporate the research, writing, and library skill goals outlined in the guide.

The South Brunswick Sixth-Grade Performance Assessment has had a significant impact on the library program and is allowing us to move into a new pattern of service, teaching, and collaboration, long talked about, but until now, never realized.

	Research & Writing	Library Skills	Oral Presentation	Visual Presentation
Third-Grade	Research at knowledge level ("list") Answer specific questions using encyclopedias/books Expository writing project	Encyclopedias—gen. info. Table of contents/Index Understanding fiction/nonfiction Location of fiction Guide words	Current events to class Present expository project to one-to-one partners	Create one visual to coordinate with assigned class project.
Fourth-Grade	Research at comprehension level ("describe," "explain") Write descriptive paper, using at least one source	Card catalog Biography Encyclopedia index Simple source notation Skimming Additional reference sources	At least one presentation to another class.	Create one visual to coordinate with assigned class project.
Fifth-Grade	Research at the application level ("conclude," "demonstrate") Practice assessment	Bibliographic form Use of Dow Jones, CD-ROM, etc. Formulation of researchable questions Periodical indexes Dewey system Location of nonfiction	At least one presentation to unfamiliar audience.	Create two visuals to coordinate with written projects.
Sixth-Grade	Formulation of research hypothesis at the evaluation level ("evaluate," "defend," "justify") Write one research paper in addition to sixth-grade assessment.	Reinforcement of all previous skills at higher level	Between Oct. and Feb.: critiqued presentation of one research project. (Using sixth-grade assessment oral presentation scale.)	Prepare coordinating/relevant visual for all research projects.

Fig. 12.6. Research, Writing, and Library Skills Goals for Each Grade Level.

Index